UP THE LADDER IN A SKIRT

Solidifying Your Leadership, One Bold Step at a Time

MAGGIE GEORGOPOULOS

Author: Maggie Georgopoulos
Title: Up the Ladder in a Skirt
ISBN: 978-1-77204-478-2
Category: BUSINESS & ECONOMICS/Women in Business

Publisher: Black Card Books
Division of Gerry Robert Enterprises Inc.
Suite 214, 5-18 Ringwood Drive
Stouffville, Ontario, Canada, L4A 0N2
International Calling: 1 647 361 8577
www.blackcardbooks.com

Printed in the United Kingdom

Table of Contents

Testimonials

Foreword

Introduction....1

Rung 1: What You Want IS What You Get....5

Rung 2: Personal Preferences....13

Rung 3: They Are Going to Find Me Out!....25

Rung 4: Get Noticed Using the Art of Saying No....33

Rung 5: Stereotypes....39

Rung 6: You as Part of a Team....49

Rung 7: Looking After Yourself....61

Rung 8: Mental Health....73

Rung 9 Mentor or Coach? That Is the Question....85

Rung 10: Which Ladder Is the Best Ladder for You?....97

Rung 11: Whose Ladder Is It Anyway?....103

Acknowledgements....107

Website: www.uptheladderinaskirt.com
Email: maggie@uptheladderinaskirt.com
Phone Number: +44 (0) 7511 234 829

Testimonials

"Look around you in the world of politics, business, even sport, and you'll see proof that women are not on the rise—they have already risen. Almost unnoticed, they have been fulfilling their potential, and stepping into their power for more than a decade.

Through this book, Maggie Georgopoulos, shares how this quiet revolution has been achieved, and how success in any walk of life, is not some special gift for the few, or just the domain of men, but an achievable goal for anyone with passion, and determination to climb their own personal ladder.

Thinking back to my own career, I found myself nodding in agreement, laughing out loud and even getting a little moisty-eyed at times. I highly recommend *Up the Ladder in a Skirt* as a powerful call to action, for any woman who wants to fulfil her potential, and any man involved in a business looking to retain its female talent. Do yourself a favour, and read it."

—Marianne Page
Creator of The McFreedom System™
www.mariannepage.co.uk

"A powerful call to action for women and businesses alike. *Up the Ladder in a Skirt* is a great guide to embracing all that you are and using the power of this in order to climb the career ladder successfully. Maggie's book is infused with clarity, insight and wisdom from one who knows."

—Jo Rawbone
Change Agent – Scintillo
www.scintillo.com

"I loved Maggie's honest and open account including many details and stories from her own life together with other amazing women's stories and carefully researched data. Maggie Georgopoulos, reminds us that we must believe in ourselves and have the courage and determination to reach for the opportunities around us, creating them if necessary."

—Hannah Beko
Partner – Gunnercooke LLP
Founder – Authentically Speaking
www.authenticallyspeaking.co.uk
www.gunnercooke.com/team/hannah-beko

"With stories of her own life, other amazing women's stories and carefully researched data, Maggie Georgopoulos, reminds women that they have to believe in themselves and reach for the opportunities. Many women, and men, may need this advice, but I am sure that they can all profit from this book."

—Karolina Gutowski Riley
Author of *In Bound of Freedom: 7 Ways on How to Live the Life of Your Desire*
www.DieSchwelleZurFreiheit.de

"A short, sharp, succinct and infinitely relatable piece of work, Maggie Georgopoulos' *Up the Ladder in a Skirt* neatly outlines - and seeks to tackle head-on - the problems facing women looking to get ahead in the business world today. Offering a perfect balance between statistics and science, anecdotes both personal and professional, and practical exercises set to guide readers along their own journey toward success, Georgopoulos' work clearly demonstrates the difficulties still besieging women in the workplace even today, and how best to go about overcoming these barriers. She does so with an engaging narrative voice, with a wit and warmth often sorely missing from texts of a business-oriented persuasion, leaving the reader in no doubt as to the honesty, integrity and wide-ranging experience of their instructor, whose lessons are geared toward inclusion as opposed to prescription. Highly recommended both for those new to the field as well as the long-experienced, as Georgopoulos' clear and vivid account of her own journey offers fresh, useful and inspirational perspectives for all."

—Karen Anderson
Director – Adiante Leadership
www.adianteleadership.com

"Maggie Georgopoulos skilfully and quickly draws the reader into this book from the outset, and continues to surprise and instruct with her expertise, the useful and interesting tools she introduces and her honest evaluation of her own life and work experiences. Interspersed with client stories, she demonstrates the problems so many women have come across in their careers - impostor syndrome, stereotyping and Superwoman - and how to deal with them. I was particularly struck by the chapter on mental health and bipolar disorder as I know it only too well in my own family. Maggie is a 'tour de force' in the flesh as well as on paper. Don't just read this book - do the exercises. The business world needs women at the top of the ladder. And hooray for the skirt!"

—Susie Heath
Speaker, trainer, author of *Dance Your Way to the Top - Feminine Leadership Without Burning Out, The Essence of Womanhood - re-awakening the authentic feminine, The Potency of the Feminine in Business.*
www.susieheath.com

"Maggie's writing is honest and thought provoking, bringing her story to demonstrate that climbing the ladder to success is a very much a personal and individual challenge."

—Judith Andrews
Senior Associate
Hidden Gem Associates
www.hiddengemassociates.co.uk

To all the women out there who want to make a difference and to those who just want to stand in their own light, this book is inspired by you and for you.

To Tom, my rock. Without your support, so much would not have been possible, especially this book.

Foreword

This much-needed and timely book has many, many layers that will help you dig deep within yourself to find your passion, your motivation, and more about your true self.

Maggie first teaches us about those voices in our head; especially the ones that are constantly shouting out critical comments about ourselves *'You're not enough! You're 'just' a woman! You're too pushy! You're too big/small! You're too... whatever!'*

This book reminded me just how critical I was of myself sometimes, and why those negative voices were actually impeding growth in certain parts of my life.

I knew a lot about being a woman in business and how to be an effective leader, and then along came this treasure – *Up the Ladder in a Skirt* – to affirm what I knew to be true, enhance my belief in my abilities and share some fresh ideas to deal with the on-going challenges we face on a daily basis. Thanks to Maggie I can recognize faster and deal with the aforementioned 'voices' – allowing me to get back on track quicker and get back to business.

As we all know a woman is never supposed to reveal her age. But you can probably take a healthy guess at mine when I tell you – I started my career when there were no computers on desks or fax machines plugged into the wall. (I know, some of you are asking, *'What's a fax machine?')*

What I'm saying is – I've been in business for a long time.

Since the cavemen traded furs and trinkets, men have seemingly ruled the business world and then they decided that they should be the ones teaching courses on how to climb the corporate ladder. Very few of us attended leadership courses taught by a woman, especially a woman who held senior positions in major companies. Therefore, we were taught to: think like a man, act like a man, and succeed like the male role models we were told to follow.

Unfortunately, there were so many stereotypes regarding what we had to do to be a successful leader, we began believing them. We then noticed that many men 'said' they supported a woman's right and ambition to climb the corporate ladder – only to find out – they wanted to look up our skirt while we were doing it.

Maggie has taken the bull by the horns and expressed what many of us think, but felt uncomfortable saying out loud: **Women have unique needs, fears, strengths, and talents.** By changing the traits that can impede us, and celebrating our strengths, Maggie shows us how we can alter the way we are perceived by others. Even being 'one of the boys', which some women believe will help them climb the corporate ladder, can become a trap for advancement.

We women often think the way to the top is by doing everything asked of us. Maggie really hits the nail on the head when she explains how this is actually a detriment.

She makes us re-examine the way we 'think we should act' in order to prove ourselves worthy. We rarely give ourselves credit for work done, and we focus too much on the wellbeing of others. Both characteristics, while in theory sound nice, are actually doing us great harm.

In addition, Maggie addresses the female stereotypes that we abhor yet we find ourselves feeding into and even falling prey to them. I love the cute little story she shares about a time when she was a child and declared she wanted to 'marry a woman' so that she didn't have to be a housewife. Her wife could take care of the home and kids!

Whether you're a student in university, just entering the workforce, or like me, with many years of fax-less experience in business, this book will enlighten, educate and entertain you. Women of all ages and backgrounds will garner some unique wisdom from this Women's Success handbook.

So get out your pen and paper and take advantage of some of the eye-opening and creativity-inspiring exercises Maggie provides that will help you uncover more about your real self, and how you can better reach that glass ceiling, smash a hole in it and climb through the jagged hole – so you can celebrate your rightful place – at the top, right where you belong!

Every woman will see herself in some form, in *Up the Ladder in a Skirt.*

It's time to take the next step. I'm going to change into my skirt, and grab my ladder!

Deborah Turton
COO, Black Card Books
www.blackcardbooks.com

Introduction

For a child growing up in Australia in the early 1970s and '80s, there were very few female leadership role models. There were many who could show me how to be a wonderful wife and mother, but hardly any who demonstrated the kind of career a woman might aspire to follow.

Thus I was drawn to women I saw in the media, and at the time these were mainly women in politics. I was particularly attracted to Margaret Thatcher. My attraction had nothing to do with her politics, and, regardless of the leadership decisions she made in Britain, she is still one of my greatest female role models. This is because, as a small girl of 10 or 11, I saw a strong woman in charge of a country. What an inspiration this was for me!

The inspiration had little to do with how she led her country, rather, in my young pre-teen mind it demonstrated what I and many other young girls could achieve in the future. She 'told' me I could become the Prime Minister of Australia, if that was what I really wanted. As a child, I didn't see the politics, but I certainly saw what I could be if I had the ambition.

As I grew older, I discovered there were women in Australia whom I admired: Miles Franklin, the Australian author who, following in the footsteps of the Bronte sisters and other British Victorian women, chose a male-sounding name to get published, and Moira Kelly, who has spent her life working with disadvantaged children and those in refugee camps long before the current refugee crises. She is still a woman I greatly admire. Internationally, there were Mother Teresa, Eleanor Bridges, Rosa Parks and many more. In fact, when I knew where to look, there were numerous women I could emulate.

What I did discover was that, unlike my male peers in high school and university, I really needed to look for women who were in roles I aspired to or had written books I was interested in reading.

So there I was in the early 1990s, a young woman at the start of her career, recognising that, despite more publicity, it was still a very male- dominated world and there was a dearth of writing on female leadership.

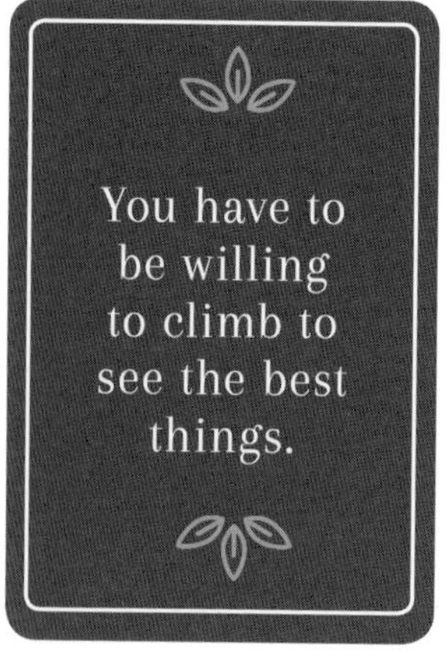
You have to be willing to climb to see the best things.

It is changing now. There are great role models out there for young girls today, from Emma Watson, with her feminist-awareness programme, 'He for She'; Baroness Michelle Mone, who has set up a multi-million-dollar business, succeeding with grace; and Angela Merkel, who, like Margaret Thatcher before her, is showing everyone you can be one of the most powerful leaders in the world on your own terms.

What is still lacking is women on the speaker circuit, motivating people to succeed. Most of all, there is a need for more books written **by** women **for** women. A Goodreads survey of 40,000 British people demonstrated they prefer to read books written by their own sex.

My own frustration, as more and more males consider themselves the most appropriate people to train women on how to expand their horizons and become leaders, and the argument that gender-specific training is unnecessary, has led to *Up the Ladder in a Skirt* – the book and the programme.

It is important to address different personalities, not just gender, and create an environment where women can see others who are successful out there inspiring them, or writing books they really want to read.

This book is one of the greatest, hardest journeys of my life. When living and working in South Korea, sight-seeing was top of my agenda when I had the chance. One thing that my Korean friends and colleagues liked to say was:

'You have to be willing to climb to see the best things.'

Whilst they were referring to the best sights South Korea has to offer, I believe this quote succinctly sums up what we all need to do to succeed in life.

Whilst writing this book, I have had to face many personal demons. The result is that my intended simple business book has taken far longer than originally planned. At one stage I downed tools for nearly four months. Every time I tried to write, the demons in my head interfered. This is, therefore, an account of my journey; one which I hope will inspire you too.

Included are stories about my own career, personal challenges and successes that will hopefully strike a chord within you. If this means facing up to things you have been trying to ignore or postpone, or recognising things that have been blocking your progress, perhaps never considered before, this is the time to face them.

Up the Ladder in a Skirt is not just about career building, or leadership growth, or any of the other aspects we have to think about regarding business or employment. It is also about personal understanding, personal growth and personal development. It means looking beneath the surface into yourself and getting to your heart song; knowing your passion.

Having introduced you to the 'voices in my head' and how they have affected me, it is time to consider the many aspects that affect the ability of so many of us to 'climb up the ladder in skirts'.

RUNG 1

What You Want IS What You Get

The 'Voices' in Your Head

There are various talks, books and training programmes on mind over matter. This is because what you continue to tell yourself subconsciously is what will come to be. At the simplest level, continually telling yourself you can't do something means you won't succeed.

Names such as: Pixie,
Auntie 'so and so'
and even evil me!

I have been as guilty of this as anyone. A voice in my head kept on telling me I was no good, that I would never be able to do things I dreamed of and, strangely enough, it became a self-fulfilling prophecy.

I have heard many names for the 'voices' in your head. You may have heard them too. Names such as: Pixie, Auntie 'so and so' and even evil me! Whatever you call them, these 'voices' are often based on perceptions of the world built up during our childhood and carried into adulthood. If there is a person you attribute the 'voices' to they would probably be astonished. It is amazing how the mind of a child can interpret quite innocent words and actions.

My 'voice' is my mum's. If she was to read this book, I know she would be shocked at this. My mum, in real life, is nothing like the 'voice'. As a rational, thinking adult, I know that. But as a child, I didn't see things in the same way.

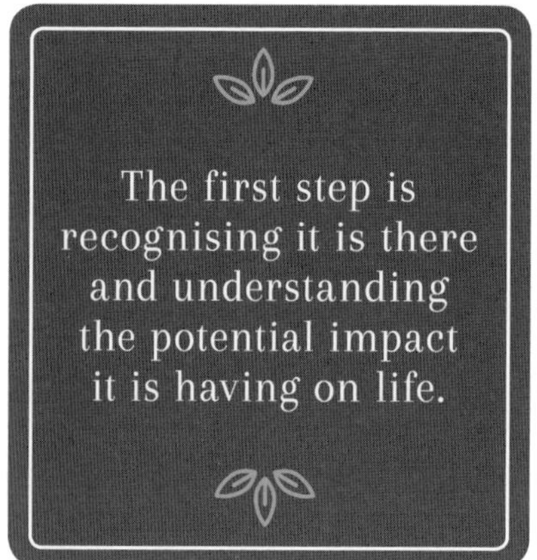
The first step is recognising it is there and understanding the potential impact it is having on life.

This voice could be described as 'negative speak'. Whenever I start a new project or apply for a new role this voice is there in the background, constantly telling me I am not good enough. Inevitably, I consider this is the case, and so anything, even marginally negative, that I see and hear confirms this. Thus, even as an adult, if I hear concern in my mum's voice, I interpret this as implying I am going to fail rather than recognising the genuine care and concern it really is. Now that's irrational!

What can anyone do to counter this?

The first step is recognising it is there and understanding the potential impact it is having on life. Now, before you start allowing that inner voice to interfere, stop! I'm not making this simple. Your voice does have a real basis. I understand this only too well. I don't think it is simple at all. That's why I am starting with it. It is complicated and, on its own, can create a barrier that stops you from succeeding!

Now for an exercise. You need a notebook. It can be something small, perhaps with an attractive cover, or you could use your phone or tablet. Choose what is most comfortable for you. Whenever you hear these negative 'voices' I want you to write down what is said. After you have written down what they are saying to you, counter it with a positive thought which you know to be true.

Two things will start to happen:

1. You will become conscious of the 'voices', and so you can start to take conscious control over their impact on your life and career.
2. Eventually, it will become automatic to counter negative talk with your own voice (still in your head or out loud) using a positive mantra.

What Do You Want?

When you were at school, you may have been confused about what you wanted. Thus, whilst others knew absolutely what they wanted from a young age and were very focused, you may have taken a more scenic route. I know I was like this. What everyone needs to grasp is that either way is fine. One is just a little more direct than the other.

How do we know what we want to do? It is not easy and often we discover, further down the track, that what we originally chose was not the right thing for us; nevertheless, it is always helpful to have something to focus on, especially if we are looking to climb that ladder.

It is important to know yourself.

Exercise: Satisfaction

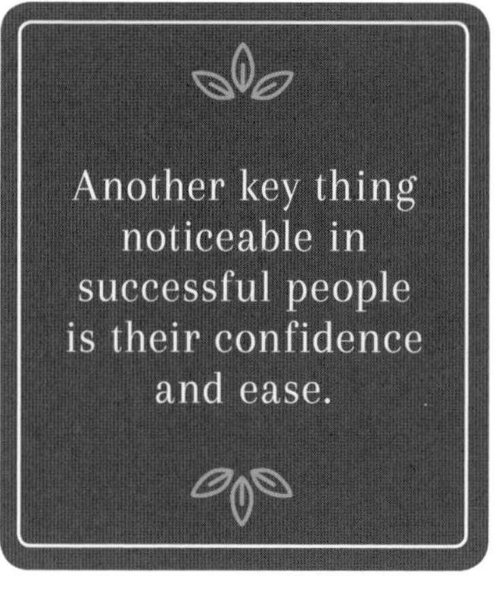

Another key thing noticeable in successful people is their confidence and ease.

For those of you who are unsure at this stage, here is a little exercise to help focus your mind. In the space below or in your notebook, make a list of the things you enjoy doing. I ask you to do this because the most successful people are doing something they love; something they are passionate about; something they enjoy and look forward to doing every day.

____

____

____

____

____

____

____

____

Now that you have done this, compare the list with your current role.

Does it match up?

Are there gaps?

If the things you enjoy match with your current career path, you will find the task of climbing the ladder much easier. If it doesn't match, then this is a good time for a review. Sandra's experience may help you.

Sandra is a woman I worked with early in my coaching/entrepreneurial career. She is extremely successful. At the time I was working with her, she was on the board of directors of a manufacturing company supplying automotive parts to companies like Toyota Australia, Ford and Holden. Her undoubted abilities had been rewarded with a six-figure salary and a company car, and she was on track to achieve the goals she had set herself in university.

However, there was a problem. Sandra was always sick, she didn't take time off, and her private life was almost non-existent because she was too exhausted to do anything. She found reasons not to update her CV, thus avoiding taking the next step up the career ladder. She even dreaded going to work. Her five-year relationship had broken up; she preferred to stay at home rather than socialize, and constantly suffered from minor illnesses. Her life was effectively in meltdown.

During a number of coaching sessions, it transpired that her apparently successful career was not what she really wanted to do. This was a 'light bulb' moment. All her life she had been following her mother's dream, and succeeding. Now, although she hadn't realised it, she had reached the point in her life where she was tired, stressed and disillusioned because she was actually climbing someone else's leadership ladder!

Sandra resigned from her job, took time out to assess what she really wanted to do and now has a highly successful career in the charitable sector.

What we tell our minds to do, even subconsciously, will become who we are!

What You Get

So far, I have concentrated on the choices we make, both consciously and subconsciously, and how they have a major influence on where we start and where we end up going in our careers. Another key thing noticeable in successful people is their confidence and ease. It may not always seem obvious, but it shows as a twinkle in their eyes when they are onto something; passion in their voices when they speak about things; the fact they don't consider what they are doing is a chore.

In complete contrast, if you are unhappy with your life, have trouble getting up in the morning, don't want to go to work, feel constantly grumpy, are that person who bites others' heads off just because they are in a good mood, you are in the wrong place.

If you are in this situation, it is very important to go back to the steps above and check if it is what you are doing or where you are going that is the problem.

Knowing yourself makes this much easier to do. We are going to look more closely at other aspects of your life to help build your success as a leader. Eventually you will find yourself climbing the ladder, all the way to the top!

Key Strategies Required to Climb the Ladder

- Know what the 'voices' in your head are saying and be conscious of them. Use this awareness to change the story you are telling yourself.
- Know what makes you happy at work and make sure your current role is giving you that. If it isn't, think how you can change the situation.
- Be aware that what you do and tell yourself is the 'inner roadmap' your subconscious will use to guide you.

Scan this code to get a discount for your
MBTI Personality Indicator Questionnaire.
www.magsinspires.com/MBTI/Bookdiscount

RUNG 2

Personal Preferences

We all like to do things in a particular way. It may be something as simple as how you make your sandwiches or something more complex, such as how you like to travel to work or what music you enjoy. We happily acknowledge these differences in one another, but often fail to do so when it comes to differences in the workplace.

Why is this important?

If we understand how we like to work as an individual, it is easier to understand why we are better at some tasks than others; why we behave in certain ways, and even why others react to us in the way they do.

Understanding Personal Preferences

There are many tools available to help us understand why we like to work the way we do. You don't need a personality profile like Myers-Briggs, Insights or Disc, to know your taste in music or books, but it can be useful in helping us as individuals to understand how we operate in the workplace.

A classic example from my career comes from when I began working as the group human resource manager for a large agricultural company in Australia. When I arrived at work every morning, I passed through the reception area dishing out a series of tasks. Upon reaching my office I got on with my work. Often, I arrived before everyone else and came out and told everyone what needed to be done when they arrived. It never occurred to me to greet anyone, perhaps comment on something, like a new hairstyle, or say anything about how they were fulfilling their tasks.

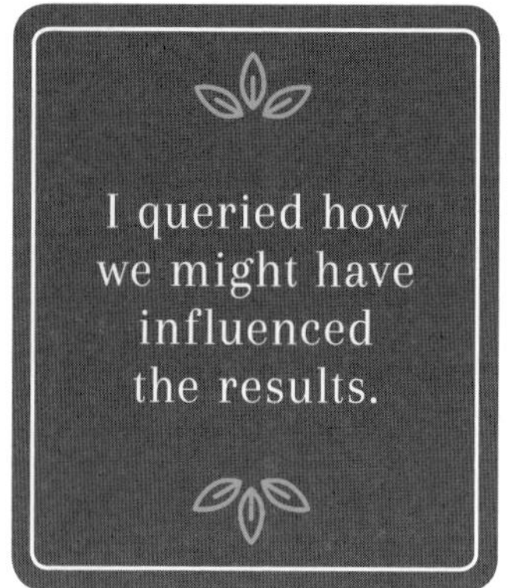
I queried how we might have influenced the results.

After a couple of months working in my first major leadership role in human resources, I decided it would be useful to do a leadership course. My employer agreed that, if I paid for the course, I could attend on workdays. After the first day, I realised I was looking at things in a totally different way. This was the start of my love of all things involving developing leaders – another whole story in itself.

Before the course, we were asked to do a number of psychometric tests, one being the Myers-Briggs Type Indicator (MBTI). When we got the results on the first morning I queried how we might have influenced the results. Apart from this I watched, listened and assimilated what I heard.

In the afternoon we were put into two groups based on a section of the profile. This was the first time I really spoke up. The outcome of the exercise left me totally mortified!

We had been split based on our personal preference for doing things, based on thinking logically around things or around people. I stood out as having a very strong preference for thinking logically around things; otherwise known as a thinking (T) preference in MBTI. This is not a bad thing, but when it was pointed out that I had convinced our group to make decisions based on financial needs, with human needs coming a poor second, I was ashamed.

That night I reflected on the events of the day. Although my instinct was to argue against what had been revealed, I realised it actually described me rather well. The way I interacted with people spoke volumes and explained how they interacted with me.

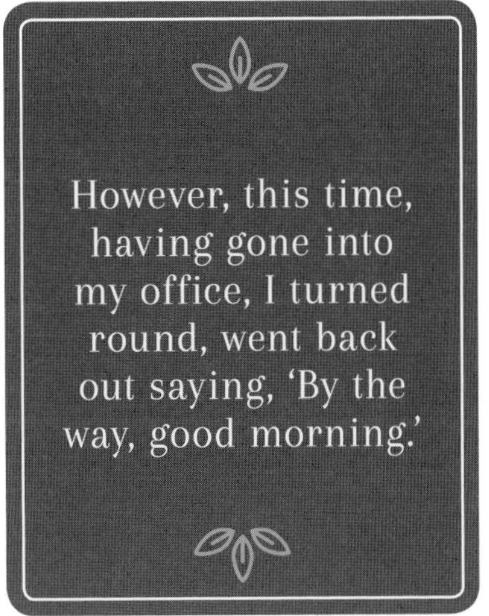
However, this time, having gone into my office, I turned round, went back out saying, 'By the way, good morning.'

When I returned to work I walked through giving out tasks as usual. However, this time, having gone into my office, I turned round, went back out saying, 'By the way, good morning,' before going back to get on with my work. On that first occasion I caused some confusion and entertainment, but from then on the dynamic of the office changed, with everyone working together as I started making more effort to reflect on how my actions and decisions impacted my colleagues.

Thinking about how you like to work as an individual can help, and how it impacts on your colleagues can improve working relationships a great deal. I am sure there have been people you worked with in the past you were frustrated by. Why did it take them so long to do something? Why didn't they understand what you were asking them to do? Often this wasn't just a case of poor communication, but because your way of doing things and theirs just didn't match.

I would recommend you take a personality profile such as the MBTI – the one I recommend, although there are many others you can use. Here is a simple exercise you can start with to help you understand more clearly the way you prefer to work.

Please remember this is a guide, not an absolute. If this exercise makes you think, I would recommend you to work with a certified practitioner and do things properly.

Exercise: Your Personality Preferences

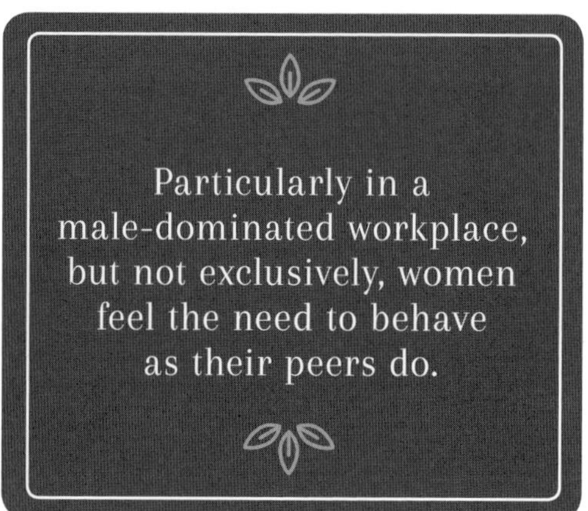

Particularly in a male-dominated workplace, but not exclusively, women feel the need to behave as their peers do.

In the following tables, choose the list you feel describes you best. When you have your three-letter combination, you will be able to find your basic type in one of the 16 boxes in the final table. Remember, this is only a brief explanation of your preferences.

Are You Introverted or Extroverted?

Choose the option that best fits you (some things may not fit, but we are looking for the best fit here).

<table>
<tr><td>• I am the life and soul of the party.
• I enjoy being the centre of attention.
• I am skilled in handling social situations.
• I like to be where the action is.
• I make new friends easily.
• I recharge best from being around other people.</td><td>• I am quiet around strangers.
• I don't like to draw attention to myself.
• I don't like to go out at the weekends.
• I like to work independently.
• I often enjoy spending time by myself.
• I recharge best by being in a quiet space on my own.</td></tr>
<tr><td>Option A</td><td>Option B</td></tr>
</table>

What Drives You?

Choose the option below that best fits you – remember you may not resonate with every item in a list.

• Easily distracted by new thoughts/ideas • Never seem to be settled, especially with others • Often like to work on new and different things • Have a sense of adventure • Like new, rich and unique experiences • Creative • Adaptable • Curious • Insightful • Warm • Loyal	• Lots of new thoughts and ideas • Can be decisive and get things done • Don't like change/takes time to adapt to change • Persistent • Loyal • Insightful • Curious/inquisitive • Like to plan • Encouraging • Enthusiastic
Option A	**Option B**
• Focused in the here and now • Like to experience the world and all that is in it • Playful • Organised but flexible • Open • Go along with others • Put others first • Live in the present • Listener	• Like structure, schedules and routines • Practical and in the moment • Organised and strategic • Dependable • Realistic • Disciplined • Careful • Driven
Option A	**Option B**

How Do You Make Your Decisions?

Once again, select the option that best fits you.

Option A	Option B
• Like to analyse things • Like to deal with facts • Value logic • Carefully analyse the pros and cons of a situation • Objective in decision making	• Like to consider other people's feelings when making a decision • Make decisions based on circumstance • Always look at the personal impact of the decision • Subjective in decision making

Results:

Responsible Realist (ADA) Quiet, serious and very responsible. Values traditions and loyalty.	Practical Helper (ADB) Quiet, friendly and responsible. Notices and remember specifics about people they care about.	Insightful Visionary (ABB) Seeks meaning in all things. Wants to understand what motivates people.	Conceptual Planner (ABA) Strong drive for implementing ideas and achieving goals.
Logical Pragmatist (ACA) Analyses what makes things work and can organise large amounts of data.	Versatile Supporter (ACB) Quiet, friendly, sensitive and kind. Enjoys the present moment.	Thoughtful Idealist (AAB) Seeks to understand people and help fulfil their potential. Curious and quick to see possibilities.	Objective Analyst (AAA) Seeks to develop logical explanations for everything that interests them. Quiet, contained and analytical.

Energetic Problem Solver (BCA) Take a pragmatic approach. Enjoy material comforts and style.	Enthusiastic Improviser (BCB) Outgoing, friendly and accepting. Exuberant lover of life and people.	Imaginative Motivator (BAB) Warmly enthusiastic and imaginative. Spontaneous, flexible and can improvise confidently.	Enterprising Explorer (BAA) Quick, alert and outspoken. Resourceful in solving new and challenging problems.
Efficient Organiser (BDA) Practical, realistic and matter-of-fact. Clear set of logical standards.	Supportive Contributor (BDB) Warm-hearted, conscientious and cooperative. Wants harmony in life.	Compassionate Facilitator (BBB) Warm, empathetic, and responsible. Finds potential in everyone and provides inspiring leadership.	Decisive Strategist (BBA) Frank, decisive, and notices inefficacies. Enjoys expanding knowledge and sharing it with others.

Note: this is a very simplified version based on the MBTI, if you really want to work this out, please get a proper professional assessment and coaching. Names for the types have been taken from OPP's summary of the MBTI types.

Play to Your Strengths

Particularly in a male-dominated workplace, but not exclusively, women feel the need to behave as their peers do. This can cause feelings of unhappiness or dissatisfaction, and can also mean you fail to reach your true potential; you might even leave your job, and as a result step off the career ladder.

To move forward in your career, you need to play to your strengths and be clear about your choices. It is not unusual to be told that working harder will enable you to improve. This can have two outcomes. First, you may work even harder to prove you are really capable; regardless of the effects this may have on other areas of life. Second, you just give up. Of course, I would never advocate not working to improve things. I am simply suggesting we need to learn to prioritise – working on improving our strengths, but also recognising what we are not so good at. It is important to understand that this does not signify weakness. Looking at ways to boost these areas will benefit everyone.

One woman I worked with when I ran a leadership retreat wanted to enhance her success leading the membership development team of the large NGO she was employed by. Part of my programme always looks at people's strengths. Jenny was a vibrant outgoing individual who was able to connect with people almost immediately. This vibrancy was the reason the president of her local organisation had approached her to take on leadership of the project. In their opinion, she was the ideal person to build membership.

It is always important to check the job description and ensure it really matches your strengths. Jenny's strength was in connecting to people and getting them excited about something. On the surface, it certainly seemed she was in the right role. The problem was that under her leadership, membership was diminishing rather than increasing.

A thorough survey of the tasks involved in leading the team demonstrated that this was actually not a role that played to her strengths. The role actually required somebody with strong organisational skills. It was about following up membership payments, rather than attracting people to join the organisation.

After working through Jenny's key strengths, it became clear she was better suited to a role that promoted her as the face of the organisation and helped attract people. Somebody with organisational skills could then undertake the administrative role, ensuring the new member was nurtured and stayed connected.

Playing to Jenny's strengths meant it was possible to restructure her team, ensuring her skills were exploited effectively. Positive outcomes followed. Membership multiplied and connections grew as everyone in the team felt they were valued for their contributions.

How Do You Recognise What Your Strengths Are?

If you understand how you work most effectively, you can start to recognise them. One way to find out is by taking a personality profile, like the MBTI referred to in the last chapter, or you could do a specific Strengths Finder exercise.

In the case study above, you should have been able to identify why the outcomes Jenny achieved did not match her overall personality. After taking a Strengths Exercise, she understood why she struggled so much.

Exercise: Your Strengths

This simple exercise should help you recognise the strengths and weaknesses in your current role. In the space below or in your notebook, record all the key tasks involved in it. In the column beside it, list how you feel when you are doing each task: Will you stop other things to complete it or put it aside until it has to be done? Once you have completed this exercise you should have a clearer picture of your strengths. On my leadership courses, students are taken through a more detailed version.

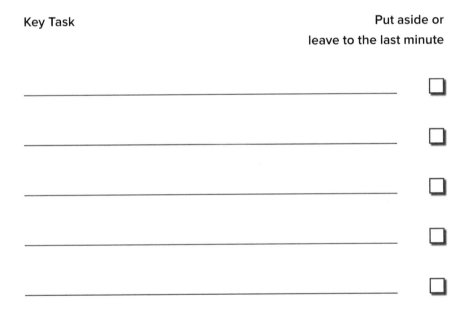

Key Task	**Put aside or leave to the last minute**
______________________________	☐
______________________________	☐
______________________________	☐
______________________________	☐
______________________________	☐

If you are in a position to delegate, you can start allotting tasks you like to avoid to others in your team who demonstrate these skills. If you don't have this option, start organising your time so tasks that you aren't happy with aren't always put off to the last minute, perhaps even left unfinished, when deadlines are imminent. You will then work more effectively, get better results, and put yourself in a position where your strengths will be noticed.

By delegating, you can begin to structure your working life, and begin to climb the corporate ladder effectively.

You can analyse your strengths. The way we prefer to perform tasks is often related to our strengths, so if you are still unsure, here is a final Strengths Exercise that should help.

Exercise: Matching Strengths with Type

From the Pretences Exercise, match your three-letter code to the appropriate box below to discover the strengths that you can use effectively.

Responsible Realist (ADA) Orderly and organised Handles criticism well Good listener	Practical Helper (ADB) Good listener Eager to serve Great organisation	Insightful Visionary (ABB) Good listener Communication Insightful	Conceptual Planner (ABA) Highly intelligent Honours commitments Independent
Logical Pragmatist (ACA) Self-reliant Handles conflict well Efficient	Versatile Supporter (ACB) Loyal and committed Laid back and adaptable Good listener	Thoughtful Idealist (AAB) Loyal Loving and caring Reads others' feelings	Objective Analyst (AAA) Laid back Not demanding Imaginative and creative
Energetic Problem Solver (BCA) Flexible and tolerant Focuses on the present Learns by doing	Enthusiastic Improviser (BCB) Working with others Uses common sense Adaptable	Imaginative Motivator (BAB) Fun and optimistic Reads others well Communication	Enterprising Explorer (BBA) Communicative Laid back Generates ideas

Efficient Organiser (BDA) Loyal and committed Social and enthusiastic Born leader	Supportive Contributor (BDB) Focuses on others' needs Money management Honours commitments	Compassionate Facilitator (BBB) Communicative Affectionate and loyal Honours commitments	Decisive Strategist (BBA) Excellent with money Takes criticism well Goal setting

There is so much you can do once you recognise your preferences and strengths that will help you improve your work and daily life. This book can point you in the right direction. Now you are equipped with a greater understanding of how you prefer to work, it is time to examine one of our biggest problems as women – taking on superpowers.

Key Strategies for Climbing the Ladder

Understand what your personal preferences are, the way they affect the decisions you make and how you communicate with others.

Know what your strengths are so you can use them effectively.

Recognise your preferences and strengths and use them to get the best out of yourself, and get noticed.

RUNG 3

They Are Going to Find Me Out!

"You gain strength, courage and confidence by every experience in which you really stop to look fear in the face. You are able to say to yourself, 'I lived through this horror. I can take the next thing that comes along.'"

—Eleanor Roosevelt

I have an amazing female mentor. Dr Joanna Martin is an extremely successful businesswoman, but this is not the reason I think she is amazing. It is because she is not afraid to stand up and address a roomful of strangers, sharing her failures just as openly as her successes. When addressing women about taking their rightful place as leaders in their communities, Joanna carries out an activity on being Superwoman.

Joanna pulls out a cape and a pair of large underpants, pulls the underpants on over her slacks and puts the cape over her shoulders. Then she introduces Superwoman to the world. Every woman in the room has a bit of a giggle, but I am convinced many will also feel a little bit uncomfortable, just as I did, because they are suddenly faced with a parody of themselves.

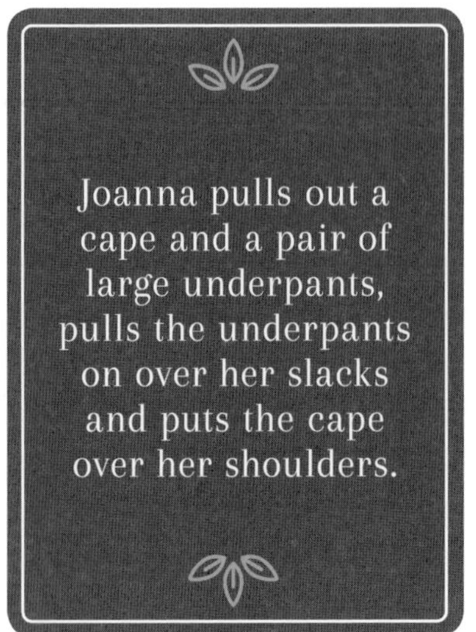
Joanna pulls out a cape and a pair of large underpants, pulls the underpants on over her slacks and puts the cape over her shoulders.

Joanna continues with a story. Starting with an incident from her childhood, she uses further events from her teens and early adulthood. As each event in the story unfolds, she borrows a pair of reading glasses from someone in the audience and puts them on and by the end she cannot see very well at all!

She uses this activity to demonstrate what happens to our confidence as we go through life. Incidents that make us feel even slightly inadequate contribute our future behaviour in similar circumstances. For example, 'If I do this, then something bad will happen,' or 'If I do that I will be loved and appreciated.'

How does this link to confidence?

At a very basic level, confidence comes from a feeling of emotional security because you believe in yourself. As you mature, anything that makes you think a particular action will have negative consequences starts to undermine your self-belief, and will become one of those 'voices in your head.'

Superwoman

Superwoman is a persona many women start to develop in their formative years. The compelling but highly unrealistic expectation is that, as women, we must be all things to all people. Our role models appear to have it all, so we consider we must excel in our careers; nurture our intimate relationships; care for our children and our aging parents; be generous towards others; maintain an exciting social life; remain physically fit;

appear youthful and attractive; and pursue superior, personal goals. In our minds, being anything less is frequently equated with failure. We mistakenly assume that other women are juggling careers, family responsibilities, social activities, and volunteer commitments successfully and therefore feel inadequate if we aren't doing the same.

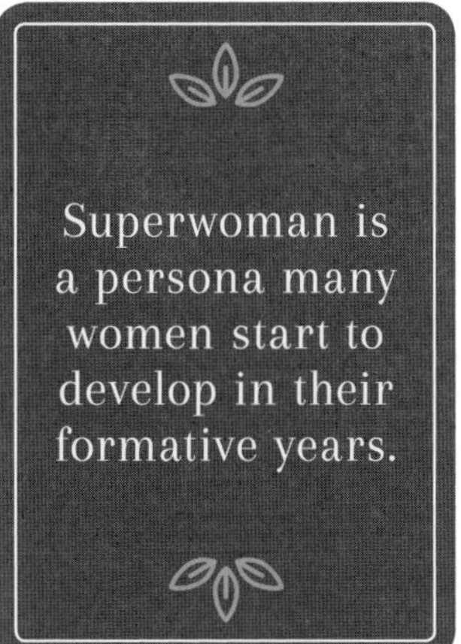
Superwoman is a persona many women start to develop in their formative years.

These are the 'glasses' of perception that cause our vision to be unfocused, but we don't recognise this. Instead, we consider ourselves failures because we aren't achieving everything. This is a huge blow to our confidence and we start feeling inadequate. Those 'voices' take over, telling us we are incompetent.

Whilst researching this book, I encountered some amazing women. One was Carey-Ann. I believe she is a great role model. As we talked about her successful career, we discussed some of the things she had done along the way.

Carey-Ann really is someone we can all admire. At one stage she was on a board of directors, had a young family and was the breadwinner. You might say she had it all. However, she decided to undertake an entirely different role when her family came along. She stopped being the breadwinner and took on a 100% commission-based role. This meant being Superwoman.

Juggling family, career and the lifestyle and hours that went with it, caused a brain injury. Having taken her eye off her personal ball, she had failed to react to the signals her body was sending her. Carey-Ann collapsed.

Once she was fit again, Carey-Ann, having learned a valuable lesson, rebuilt her business, adjusted her work-life balance and recognised it is perfectly acceptable not to be Superwoman. She is still somebody to be admired but for a totally different, but equally successful, commendable reason.

Impostor Syndrome

Impostor Syndrome is considered to be more prevalent in women, although this is debateable. Making every effort to be Superwoman, with those persistent 'voices' continually suggesting you simply aren't good enough, means you feel you are living a lie and will eventually be unmasked.

Many high-profile successful women, including Oprah Winfrey and Sheryl Sandenberg, admit to feeling like this.

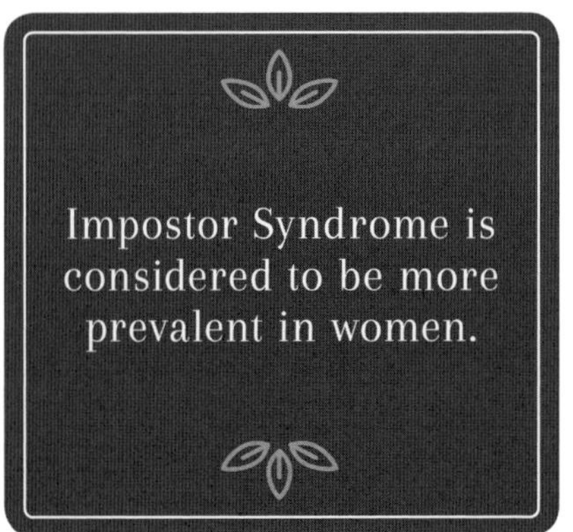
Impostor Syndrome is considered to be more prevalent in women.

The problem with Impostor Syndrome is that despite everything demonstrating how able we are, we tend to dismiss this as luck, timing or the support others have given us. We are continually under the impression that sooner or later, we will be exposed. It could manifest itself like this:

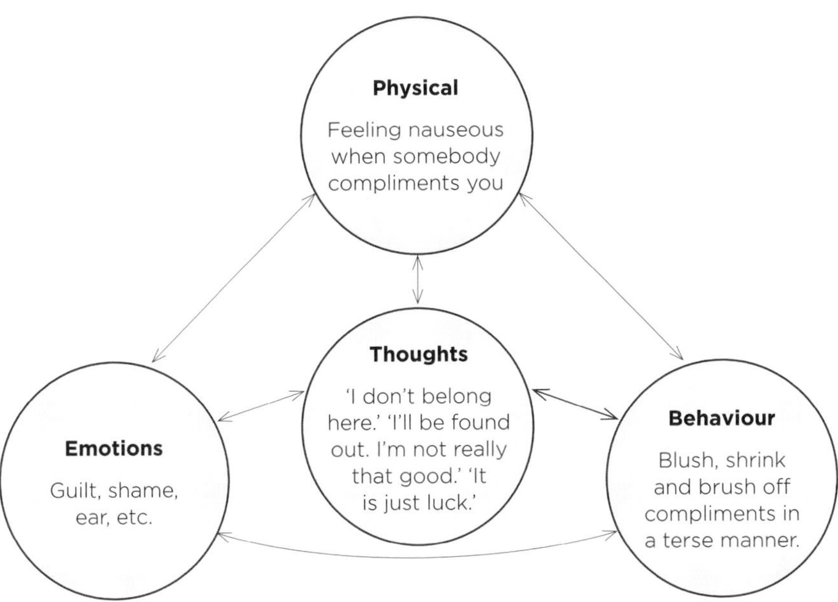

This is only one example. The thoughts, behaviour, emotions and physical interactions will be different in each individual.

Building Your Confidence

Confidence cannot be learned. Confidence is a state of mind. Confidence comes from feelings of well-being, acceptance of your body and mind (self-esteem), and belief in your own ability, skills and experience.

How can you build it up?

To build up confidence and counteract phenomena such as Impostor Syndrome, you need to be aware of some key things:

- Your strengths and weaknesses
- Everyone makes mistakes
- Compliments – how to accept them and how to give them
- How to accept criticism and use it as a learning experience
- The need to aim for a positive outlook

Exercise: The 'Voices' in Your Head

On the first rung of the ladder we talked about the 'voices' in your head and how they could affect your perceptions. For the next exercise, you need to tag this page in your book or set aside a page in your notebook. Tomorrow, whenever you have a negative thought about something you are doing, record it.

The 'voices' say:

At the end of the day, take five minutes to read through your list and identify the theme that is emerging.

Write the theme here or highlight it in your notebook:

Theme:

Now you have a key theme you need to devise a strategy to counteract the 'voices'.

Here is one method to help, but be aware there are many ways to do this and you need to find the one that works best for you.

Every time the Voice comes into your head, acknowledge what it is saying and counter it with a key fact that disproves what it is saying. You can only do this effectively if you recognise your achievements. This will be hard for some of you. However, it is one of the best ways to recognise what you can accomplish and to understand your capabilities are not just luck!

Achievements:

Things won't change overnight. Whilst it is possible to be very successful with all this in place, it doesn't stop 'burn out'. It is important to avoid burning out by looking after yourself, and acknowledging areas where you have the tendency to take on too much.

Now we have learned how Superwoman works, let's look at teaching her to say 'No'.

Key Strategies to Help You Climb the Ladder

- Watch out for Superwoman and keep her in check.
- Acknowledge that Impostor Syndrome is real.
- Building confidence by overcoming the need to be Superwoman and recognising Impostor Syndrome means always being aware of what the 'voices' in your head are saying.

No

RUNG 4

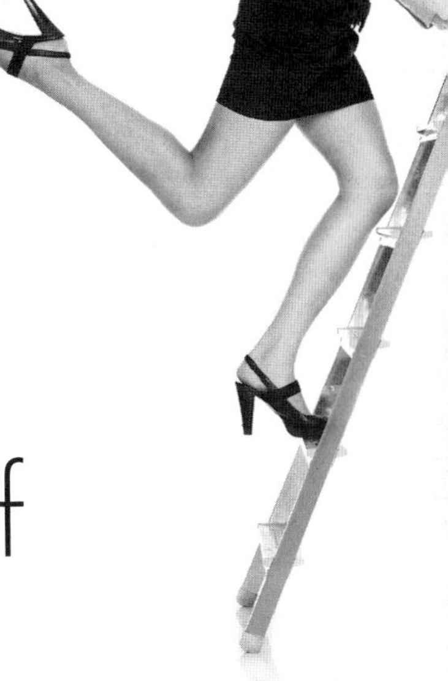

Get Noticed Using the Art of Saying No

"Ability and necessity dwell near each other."

—Pythagoras

Now you are beginning to understand your preferences and strengths, it is time to deal with another common problem for women – taking on too much!

Dr Joanna Martin demonstrated this really well with her Superwoman act. On the day I was in the audience I thought, 'I can really relate to this.'

If you have ever been guilty of trying to keep too many balls in the air, her extremely humorous presentation teaches a valuable lesson. Women have a tendency to try to be Superwomen!

Women trying to climb the corporate ladder tend to consider they will only be successful if they are doing everything asked of them, and better than everyone else!

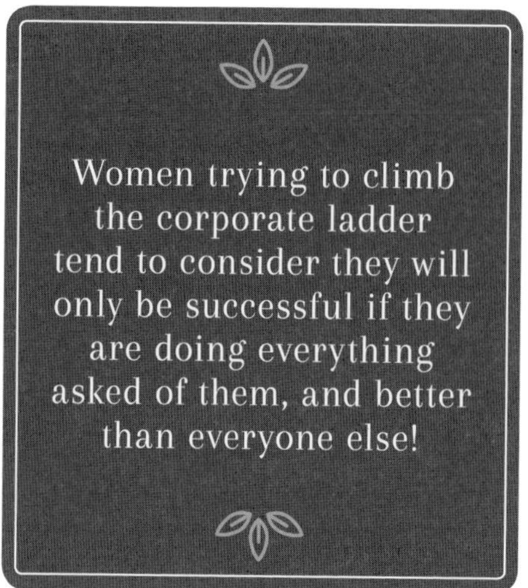
Women trying to climb the corporate ladder tend to consider they will only be successful if they are doing everything asked of them, and better than everyone else!

If you are currently balancing on this slippery rung, chances are you will fall off because when you feel stressed and exhausted, you will probably walk away. When you are drowning under a huge pile of work you probably shouldn't have taken on in the first place, you will almost certainly not be playing to your strengths. When you are so busy trying to do everything, you are in danger of being considered indispensable in your current role. You also won't have time to push yourself forward. As a result, you are likely to be overlooked for promotion.

People who know when to say yes and when to politely but firmly turn something down without implying they are being awkward are far more likely to progress. If, like them, you want to be standing firmly on your rung but find this difficult, the following tactics can help you.

Time Wasters Can Get in Your Way

My good friend Mariah worked in human resources for a large, Australian educational institution. After a couple of years, she was burning out. Mariah, a hardworking highly intelligent woman, had always been highly successful. This time she had consistently found herself doing almost all the work of her department, including training others, completing colleagues' unfinished tasks and covering vacancies. Mariah had ended up doing all this because her managers knew that if they wanted something done properly, she was just the person. The problem was that her escalating workload meant increasing hours and, almost inevitably, heightened stress levels. It wasn't long before she was going to work very early, returning home very late and having trouble sleeping. In addition, she was not eating properly or taking any exercise and was gaining weight. In a nutshell, she had no time to look after herself as her whole life revolved around work. Mariah handed in her notice.

To their credit, the company recognised she was far too good to lose and hired her back as a contractor. Now she was able to concentrate solely on the tasks she had been hired to do. Despite this, it wasn't long before Mariah decided to follow a completely different career path.

How can we avoid ending up like Mariah?

Exercise: Time Wasters

Everyone uses time wasters at times. Sometimes they are personal things, but, more commonly, they will be actions within our work setting. One example is taking on extra tasks to prove we can, even though they are not things we are good at or even interested in. Almost inevitably, and often subconsciously, we find excuses to postpone getting on with them. This is counterproductive.

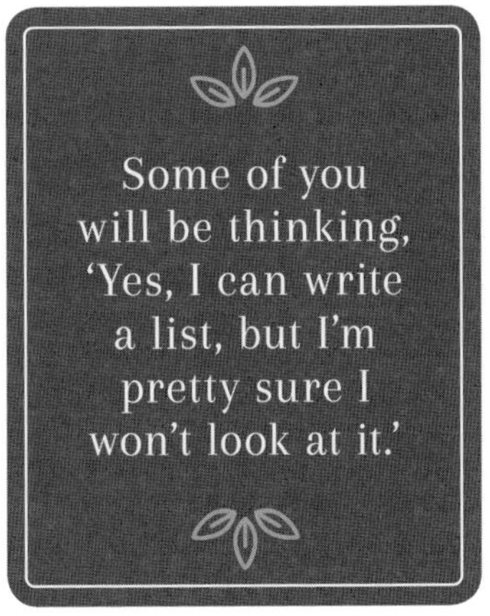
Some of you will be thinking, 'Yes, I can write a list, but I'm pretty sure I won't look at it.'

Time wasters can be things such as:

- Losing or misplacing things
- Short-term problem fixing
- Interruptions
- Telephones
- Meetings

- Being distracted from key tasks
- Perfectionism
- Task hopping
- Not delegating

I'm sure you can think of many more.

List below all the potential time wasters that you need to stop doing:

Need to stop...	I will stop doing it by...
Example: Taking on too many tasks	Creating a list of polite plausible reasons why I can't do things, whilst ensuring they don't affect my position in any way.

You now have an action plan to help you work more intelligently.

The Art of Saying NO

When we know our strengths and values and have a clear set of goals in mind, it is much easier to say no. Having a list of priorities handy is useful. I know some of you will be comfortable with this idea, whilst others, like me, will hate it. Some of you will be thinking, 'Yes, I can write a list, but I'm pretty sure I won't look at it.'

Whilst making a list may not be one of your strengths, everyone can appreciate a short exercise is worth doing if it means long-term gain. A list can help you.

When somebody asks you to take on tasks that are outside your comfort zone, don't play to your strengths and, most importantly, are likely to turn into time wasters, you can politely consult your list and ask which items can be postponed in order to fit them in.

Being polite, rather than confrontational, is the key. You're not saying you are too important or that you can't cope. Rather, you are pointing out that, with a limited number of hours in a day, something else will need to be shelved. My partner uses this technique all the time, without realising he is doing so. It is a simple and straightforward question for him, and, more often than not, his boss allocates the task to someone else or tells him clearly what can be deferred.

Exercise: The NO List (Otherwise Known as the Priority List)

Whilst we will focus on work, this can be used in all areas of your life. On the next page or in your notebook, list all the things you are currently working on. Now prioritise them, starting with the most important. It is good practice to review this list just before you leave the office, so you have your list of priorities ready for the morning. Alternatively, you can do this first thing in the morning before you check your emails or get started on anything.

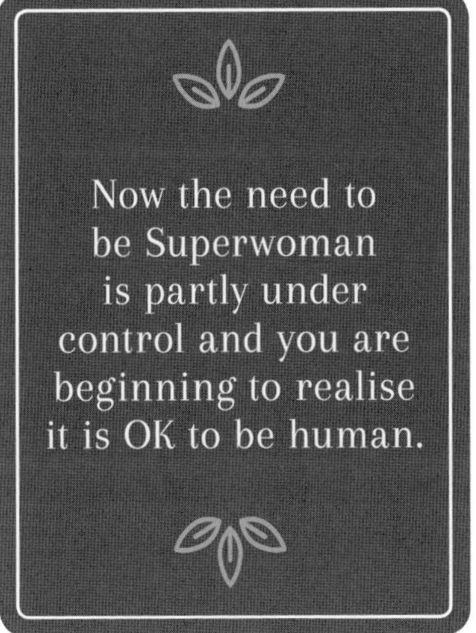
Now the need to be Superwoman is partly under control and you are beginning to realise it is OK to be human.

Task	Priority

Now the need to be Superwoman is partly under control and you are beginning to realise it is OK to be human, we need to look at another aspect of the Superwoman persona that we are often forced to take on – the persona we take on because we are stereotyped.

Key Strategies for Climbing the Ladder

- Know what your priorities are in your role and create a list to support this.
- Select actions that may be wasting your time and find ways to drop them from your daily routine.
- Put together techniques that work for you, and help you say no so you can focus your energy on your current task.

RUNG 5

Stereotypes

"Stereotyping sets Maggie Georgopoulos's teeth on edge: That professionals should be suitably attired, that academic qualifications are the truest measure of intelligence, that drought and flood cripple rural business and, her pet hate, 'that females don't make good engineers.'"

–Stephan McKenzie, the *Melbourne Weekly Magazine*, March 2004

Having talked about some of the conditioning we experience in our lives that makes us think we **must** be Superwomen, we need to examine situations that can affect how we are perceived starting with stereotypes.

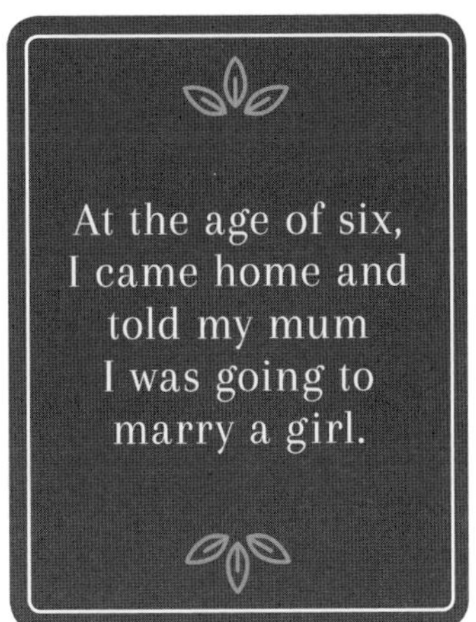
At the age of six, I came home and told my mum I was going to marry a girl.

At the age of six, I came home and told my mum I was going to marry a girl. All parents love telling stories that can cause us embarrassment in later life, and my mum is no exception. Although I hate it when she tells this story, especially to someone I am trying to impress. I'm going to share it with you as it makes a rather poignant point.

I had decided I was going to marry a girl and in my six-year-old mind it was all very clear. If I married a girl, she could stay at home and look after the children, cook the meals and clean the house while I went out to work. My friend Amber was a possibility because she liked to cook and sew! To me this was the perfect solution to a problem I was already facing – I didn't want to be a housewife.

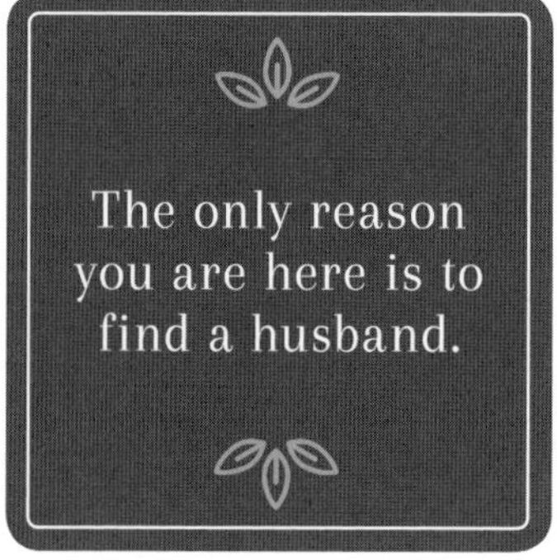
The only reason you are here is to find a husband.

This makes a delightful story for my mum to relate when she meets my friends, and inevitably, she told it when she met my partner for the first time. I still feel slightly embarrassed at my six-year-old logic. I also feel sad that, so early in my life, I was already reacting to the stereotypes I saw all around me, and beginning to make decisions based upon them. This happens to everyone throughout their lives because stereotyping continually informs and influences us.

I hate stereotypes!

But I am also guilty of feeding them and falling prey to them.

'Cooking is a woman's job,' according to my dad, who I love and is also my hero, but really? The majority of famous chefs are men, which implies cooking is basically considered as a 'woman's job' in the home.

'The only reason you are here is to find a husband,' remarked one of my fellow engineering students in my first year at university. I felt my sarcastic riposte that, if this was the case I was on the wrong course, was richly deserved.

'Once you finish your training you won't have to do any more of this rolling around in the mud stuff,' observed a female officer who had been sent out to encourage the female officer cadets at training. Her unspoken assumption that all girls hated outdoor infantry-type activities left me feeling irritated. I liked 'rolling around in the mud stuff!'

You may have had similar experiences, but yours, quite possibly, will have been quite different. Nevertheless, regardless of age, we all experience bias because of stereotyping. It isn't totally restricted to women but it does seem to happen to us more often.

> That more than a hundred years since Emmeline Pankhurst and her fellows fought their battles, we are still fighting against the stereotyping that create barriers and undermines confidence, means this is serious.

Everyday Sexism by Laura Bates highlights this. My childhood story may seem amusing when retold many years later; however, the stereotyping involved is a part of something that certainly isn't funny. There is an expectation in society that women should accept the type of comments I have included, and just get on with things. After all, they're just a bit of fun. Think about it a little further, however, and actually they are no such thing!

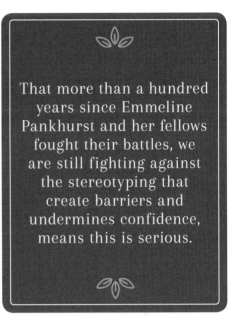

I don't believe the Suffragettes fought their battles, suffering the hardships they did so women could vote, imagined such comments as 'Now you can go back to the kitchen where you belong, love' would still be acceptable today. That more than 20 years since I left university, and more than a hundred years since Emmeline Pankhurst and her fellows fought their battles, we are still fighting against the stereotyping that create barriers and undermines confidence, means this is serious. No one should have to put up with degrading comments. It is alarming that feminism is considered to be a dirty word.

The Very Beginning – Stereotypes at School

I recently met an amazingly talented young lady called Levana. Levana is a whiz at maths and science, highly competitive and proud of the awards she has received. She is a pivotal member of an F4 team (mini go-cart-type cars). You may be surprised to learn she was only 11 when I met her in early 2016.

I met with Levana because she wants to be a mechanical engineer. I met her mother, an amazing woman and role model, at a networking event and when she discovered I was a female mechanical engineer she told me about her daughter. She said she couldn't wait to get home and tell her about me.

So let's look at Levana's story. At school, she was the unfortunate victim of bullying. This was because she loved anything technical and had a competitive streak. These are qualities that will enable her to achieve great things in the future. She is focused and knows what she wants to do with her life. This is an 11-year-old girl whose peers were telling other children she wasn't really a girl because she wasn't into wearing make-up and chasing boys. I'm sure I'm not alone in wondering why it is so important to 'doll yourself up' and fancy boys at such a young age.

Fortunately for Levana she has a strong role model in her mother; a very supportive mother too, who works in the tech industry as project manager for an animation company. Recognising Levana needed support, she took her away from the bullies' influence. Having received such positive support, Levana will almost certainly fulfil her aspiration to be an engineer in the future. In 10 years' time I'm sure she will have achieved great things.

Without her mother's positive support, her ambition might have been crushed. More often than not, the stereotyping forced upon us when we are young colours all our choices later in life, and sadly, far too often, they are choices we didn't originally aspire to.

Stereotypes and the Workplace

Curiously, it isn't very different in the workplace. Throughout my life, as some of my stories have demonstrated, I have experienced stereotyping in one form or another. I suspect this is because my generation learned to accept it – this was how things were and 'nobody likes a whiner'. Fortunately, things are starting to change at last. Today's generation are less inclined to accept it and to pretend it isn't happening. Nevertheless, the perception persists that women can't expect to follow some careers because certain occupations are still the prerogative of men.

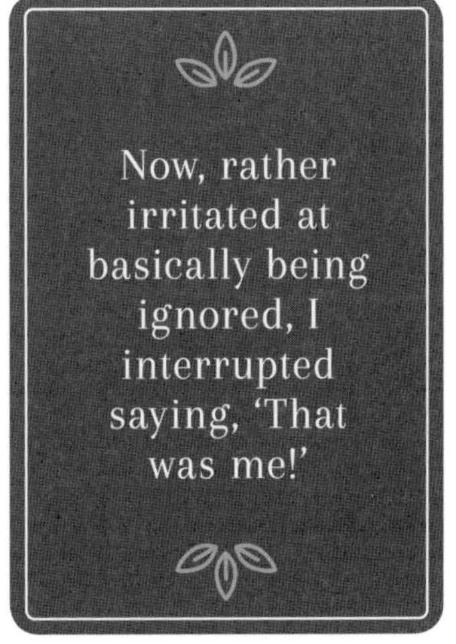
Now, rather irritated at basically being ignored, I interrupted saying, 'That was me!'

My first job after graduating was with Toyota Australia, and I am still extremely proud of this achievement. Inevitably I came up against a lot of stereotyping in this role, and as an example of what I experienced, I'm going to focus on what I encountered on my first day.

It was a big deal to have been hired by a large well-known company as a graduate engineer. As commonly happens in such organisations, the morning began in the human resources department where all the legalities were completed prior to me being allocated my role.

There were two of us. The other person, Alex, was male. The HR staff member, who was also male, turned to Alex and said, 'Congratulations on getting hired on the first round of interviews.

That was quite impressive.' Alex, looking very confused, said, 'No, I had to go through a second round of interviews.' Now, rather irritated at basically being ignored, I interrupted saying, 'That was me!' At the time it had been considered remarkable that anyone could have impressed the interviewers so much that, regardless of gender, they could beat over a hundred other candidates based on one interview, and be offered a position. It has taken me a long time to admit to this being me with pride.

It had been assumed that as the position offered was for a mechanical engineer in an automotive industry, only a male could possibly have been appointed after the first round of interviews. I don't have anything against the HR person, other than they didn't check their facts and made a fairly common assumption. The rest, unfortunately, was down to social conditioning. I wish I could say that more than 20 years later this rarely happens, but I am afraid it is still only too common.

Overcoming Stereotypes

Stereotypes are not the fault of one gender. They are something that has built up over time as a part of societal dictates. Women are just as guilty as men for allowing this to prevail. We have stereotypes that fit the characters of men and women and their suitability for certain careers. For example, men are still perceived as more assertive, and as such, are suitable for leadership roles, whilst women continue to be considered suitable for more compliant, caring assignments. This automatically comes to mind when we consider either gender. It is therefore no surprise that women are underrepresented in leadership roles and in certain industries. One of the struggles we still have is with stereotyping in some areas that has become so entrenched it has become the norm.

Now for some key steps to help overcome stereotyping and move forward:

1. Decide on who you are and how you want to be seen. Just like any key brand out there, you need the world to see you in a positive light. If you present as a 'damsel in distress' then that will be exactly what the world sees. However, if you present yourself as confident about what you want to do and where you are going, you will be seen as capable and worth employing.
2. Be genuine. It is one thing to decide who you are, but if you aren't genuine, it will be recognised quickly. Should your initial bluff succeed you will probably end up feeling unhappy and stressed. I like to wear dresses and skirts, they are comfortable. Ask any Scottish male and he will confirm this! At the same time, I am quite happy tinkering with mechanical objects, and taking part in a variety of outdoor activities. Most people would consider trousers more suitable for such activities, but I am more than happy to wear a skirt, and that is my choice. I see no need to conform to other people's ideas of suitability or fashion.
3. Be independent. This does not mean becoming Superwoman, but it does mean striving to problem-solve for yourself whenever practicable. One of the effects of stereotyping at an early age is that boys are encouraged to be independent explorers and learners, whilst girls are still far too often encouraged to be cautious. This is changing today, and as women, we have the power to influence this just as much as men. Independence at an early age enables everyone to develop key problem-solving skills that will support them in adulthood.

4. Be more aware. Our actions and words influence the way things are perceived and contribute to stereotyping. When we accept such things as 'trash talk' because it is seen as weak or whiny if we complain; or comments like, 'You run like a girl,' we contribute to the stereotype image. We need to raise awareness and discussions around this if we are to change the picture.

Alison started her career when job choices were governed far more by stereotyping. She was working in an industry which was dominated by males in leadership roles. When she started there were only males in the leadership positions in her company. The glass ceiling really did exist in that moment.

The turning point for Alison came when she had reached the level in her career where a promotion should have been hers. She had the experience, ability and expertise, but the company chose to promote a less experienced male. The stereotype in the company was that women only occupied administrative roles.

Rather than accepting defeat, Alison did what many successful women have done in the past: She identified a new area that was relatively unknown. Taking a sideways and upward step she strongly argued her case and succeeded in winning the role of Information Centre Manager. The job title was changed, however, from Manager to Administrator, as the organisation struggled with the idea of a woman occupying a management role.

Alison fought the stereotyping in small steps. She was able to take up a leadership role in the organisation. Even though the title didn't state this, the duties of the role did. She overcame preconceived ideas and moved onwards and upwards.

If we arm ourselves with a strong sense of self-awareness – how we like to work, what our strengths are and what we really want to do – it really helps overcome stereotyping. As we overcome this, we can continue to climb the ladder of success, by thinking far more in terms of how we work as part of a team. How do we play our part and influence team decisions effectively?

Key Strategies for Climbing the Ladder

- Stereotypes start at a very young age and as 'thought leaders', teachers and parents need to help eliminate them.
- Overcoming workplace stereotyping may be difficult. Overcoming other people's preconceived ideas is never easy, but it will only change because of our actions and words.
- We need to be genuine about ourselves and make sure our actions and words reflect this.

RUNG 6

You as Part of a Team

So far we have concentrated on knowing ourselves and building confidence, now we are going to look more closely at how this can influence teams you work with or lead. This is critical if you are going to climb the leadership ladder. There are some key things you need to be aware of:

- Understand your team members' preferences. This is important whether you are a team member or the leader, and will be important at all stages of your career!
- You need to avoid the 'be one of the boys' trap. This can be difficult when working in a male-dominated environment.
- Finally, you must be alert when apportioning credit in a team. Women in particular tend to favour the collaborative **'we success'** rather than the competitive **'I success'.** There is a way to include both.

Understanding the Team

Even if it seems like a wonderful idea, there is no necessity for everyone in your workplace to complete personality profiles. Remember, many people will, quite rightly, feel uncomfortable at the prospect of sharing their personal data. There are other ways to gather the data you need, including socialising and showing appropriate interest in your colleagues.

As a team member, it is always worthwhile getting to know your peers. It helps everyone work together better when members understand each other. Not everyone is comfortable making what is commonly referred to as 'small talk'. If this isn't your forte, it isn't necessary to suddenly turn into Miss Chatty or for that matter, Miss Nosey. Instead, you need to become a savvy communicator.

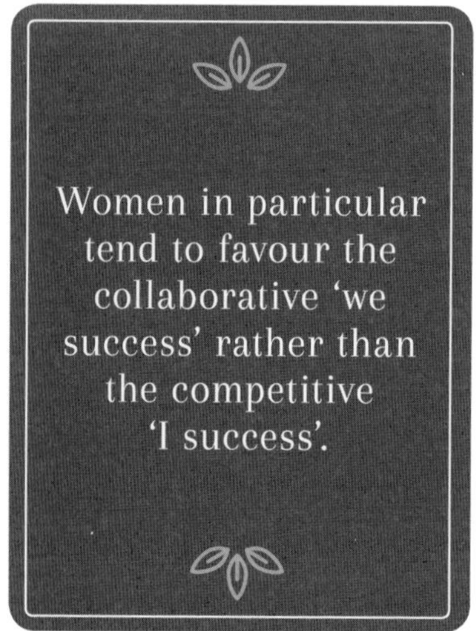
Women in particular tend to favour the collaborative 'we success' rather than the competitive 'I success'.

Getting to know your team doesn't mean spending lots of time chatting with them, but making sure you can connect with them all is a good idea and will continue to be important as you move up the leadership ladder. Always being polite and friendly when interacting with your colleagues is a very good start. It may seem a simple suggestion, but when you are wrapped up in your own world and problems, it can easily slip your mind.

Nowadays, it is very common for people to connect with their colleagues on social media. You need to be careful how you go about this if you don't want to be labelled as a cyber stalker. Nevertheless, it can be an effective way of finding out about associates' interests. Congratulating someone on an achievement or sharing a common hobby (within reason) can help you make connections.

It is also advantageous to share breaks and sometimes lunch with your team members, and, in addition, encourage social interaction away from work. Everyone needs a breathing space to keep the creative juices flowing. Remember, as a female, lunch invitations may be misinterpreted, so a team lunch is a safer option. You need to be discerning with invitations to avoid your motives being misconstrued. For instance, your colleagues may make assumptions about one-to-one dinners with clients that they consider have very little to do with your working role.

Always be aware of your team members' unspoken thoughts. Their facial expressions and body language can tell you a great deal about how comfortable they are with tasks you ask them to carry out. This will help you match tasks to the most appropriate people. It will also enable you to address your colleagues in ways they feel comfortable with, and observe how they interact with each other.

Other indicators may include outbursts if they are under pressure from constant change, whilst boredom may suggest change is needed. Frustration or misunderstanding when instructions are given may require a rethink – some may prefer step-by-step instruction, whilst others may be happier with fewer directives. Such indicators of personal work preferences are important, and the insight they provide will help you work more effectively with your team. You will almost always find it easier to work with the members of your team who like your style of management, but being aware of and adapting your style for those who struggle with it will improve the working atmosphere for all and achieve worthwhile results.

Remember, you are not taking part in a popularity contest, but achieving a good working relationship, regardless of how you may feel about some of your team on a personal level, is the key to success.

Exercise: Understanding Team Dynamics

This is a complex area, so to begin with, I would like you to complete this short exercise, which should help you understand how your team may be working together.

Think about a time when there was conflict or disagreement between you and a member of your team. What happened? How did you feel at the time? Was there anything that particularly frustrated you about the incident? Record your feelings below:

____

____

____

____

____

____

____

____

____

Is there anything that might suggest that your approach to a task differs from the approach of some of your colleagues? For instance, you may prefer to give out and receive back lots of detail, whilst they may prefer to look at the big picture and provide minimal information. Do you prefer working to a set deadline, whilst they commonly leave things to the last minute?

This would indicate some of your colleagues work more comfortably with a different set of preferences. It could also suggest that they have a different set of values.

The Boys' Club

It is only too easy to fall into the 'one of the boys' trap, especially in male-dominated working environments. Throughout my life, colleagues and friends have generally been men. In childhood, my close friends were boys, and my two best friends at university were also male.

Thus, in my early 20s I was in danger of falling into the 'one of the boys' trap. This was never my intention, I am, and always will be, a skirt- and dress-wearing female. I feel so comfortable in skirts and dresses; I have even gone hang gliding and white-water rafting in them. Originally, I didn't mind being one of the boys, but as I matured and my career advanced, I found this soubriquet offensive.

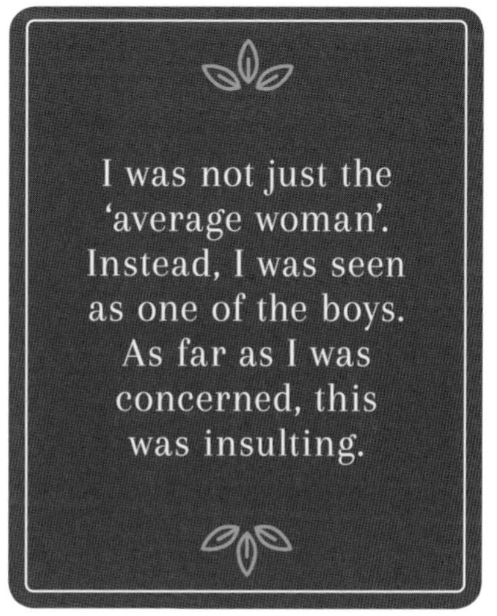
I was not just the 'average woman'. Instead, I was seen as one of the boys. As far as I was concerned, this was insulting.

My friends, work and Army Reserve colleagues considered I was not just the 'average woman'. Instead, I was seen as one of the boys. As far as I was concerned, this was insulting. I am a woman and proud of the fact, but it also occurred to me that if I was no longer seen as one of the boys, it was quite possible that my achievements would no longer attract the same kudos.

This is the reason that being seen as one of the boys can become a trap. Whilst there is nothing wrong with being one of the team, you need to be yourself and to be recognised for this. If you are comfortable doing things that are generally considered the

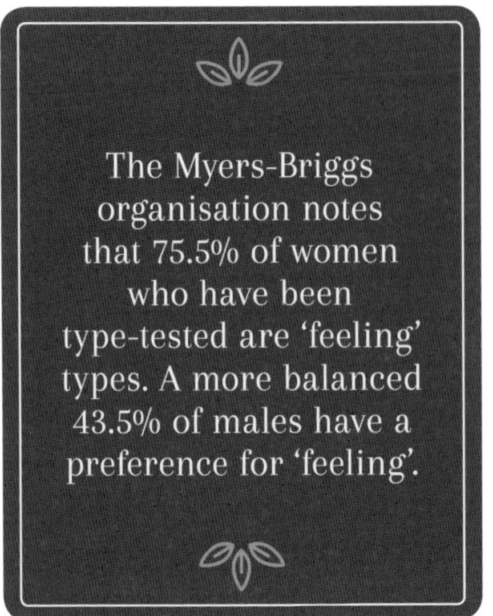
The Myers-Briggs organisation notes that 75.5% of women who have been type-tested are 'feeling' types. A more balanced 43.5% of males have a preference for 'feeling'.

prerogative of men, don't stop what you are doing; just ensure you are included and that your achievements are recognised because of who you are. This is the message I pass on to all young people I work with. If we are actually going to progress it needs to be as successful people, not as successful men or successful women. Unfortunately, there is still a lot to accomplish before current perceptions finally change.

The Cherie Blair Foundation works to support women around the world who need support in developing their careers and businesses by linking them to mentors who can provide guidance. As one of these mentors, I was put in touch with Ariana. Ariana lives in Sierra Leone. I spoke with her in early 2016, when this young mother's only child was 3 years old. Ariana was fortunate enough to receive a college level education. (Unfortunately, in Sierra Leone this is down to good fortune rather than the norm.) Ariana runs a business that would superficially appear to be stereotypically female – a childcare centre. It is important to understand that she has set the nursery up in a patriarchal society. Culturally, Sierra Leone is still very male dominated.

Ariana has faced many difficult situations as a lone female in a male-dominated field. Before setting up her current business, Ariana gave birth to her first child one afternoon whilst on a business call. The next morning, with her baby less than 24 hours old, she was back in the office dealing with the project and team she was managing. A really extreme way of showing the boys that a woman can do it all. In the end, it was the long hours that led to Ariana stepping off the corporate ladder and setting up her own business. She wanted to spend more time with her child (she has had two miscarriages at work), and being the natural leader she is, she was able to set up her own business as well as continuing to help others.

Competition versus Collaboration

The Myers-Briggs organisation notes that 75.5% of women who have been type-tested are 'feeling' types. A more balanced 43.5% of males have a preference for 'feeling'. The other preference types are balanced across gender. The very nature of making decisions based on a 'feeling' preference means it is more collaborative.

'Thinking' preferences tend to put more weight on objective principles and impersonal facts, whilst 'feeling' preferences put more weight on personal concerns and the people involved, which inevitably demands a more collaborative approach.

Of course, there are many women who don't possess the 'feeling' decision-making preference, and having the 'thinking' decision-making preference are more likely to have more competitive personalities.

At this stage, it is important to understand the dynamics.

A collaborative approach can be successful when it also includes a competitive element. We see this in highly successful female leaders who provide positive coaching and mentoring to others; highly successful female sportspeople who also keep the best interest of their team in focus; and female entrepreneurs who create highly successful businesses. Nevertheless, a collaborative nature is more predominant in women.

In general, the corporate environment seems to reward those with a competitive nature. Research by CPP, the leading body in the world on type indicators, has shown that the majority of people in leadership roles are thinking and judging types (TJ). Their preference is to promote and hire those that display similar attributes because it makes them feel comfortable. This often results in unbalanced senior leadership teams and boards because of type bias.

In *True Type Tales*, Patrick Kerwin suggests women with an MBTI preference for 'thinking' are often considered 'aggressive' in decision-making situations. The workplace culture encourages this 'thinking' characteristic which is more common in men, and, unfortunately, also more socially acceptable. Women with a 'feeling' preference may not succeed if they invoke the 'thinking' preference. It will be underdeveloped because they are uncomfortable making decisions this way.

This is a major challenge for women in leadership. Female executives are more likely to encounter negative reactions when using behaviour typical for their type than men in similar positions. This has little to do with their proficiency as leaders. On the positive side, women leaders and those with leadership aspirations will often come up against bias, so identifying and cultivating a personal leadership style will be of great assistance in overcoming barriers.

Both personality preferences and social upbringing mean women are generally more collaborative when building team confidence and creating team harmony. A collaborative approach is good; actually, it is great. It is also important to step into the spotlight and claim rightful plaudits when successful. Men aren't backward in coming forward when they have done well, and women shouldn't be either.

Claim It if It Is Yours!

Recently, I stepped in as the chairman of a not-for-profit organisation in Glasgow. Membership was dwindling and there was no obvious reason for this. The organisation valued its 'learn by doing' ethos and the opportunities this offered, but the small inexperienced team at the top now recognised that if they wanted to survive, they needed an experienced leader to guide and develop the team.

I was very happy to take on this role, and even though I am very much a thinking type, I realised the need for a collaborative unit to support these young leaders and develop their skills. Most importantly, this collaborative unit would allow them to grow in confidence.

This was so successful that I was able to step aside a year ahead of schedule, allowing one of the team members to take on the mantle of chairman. This culminated in the successful hosting of a traditional dinner for a large number of Glasgow's business elite.

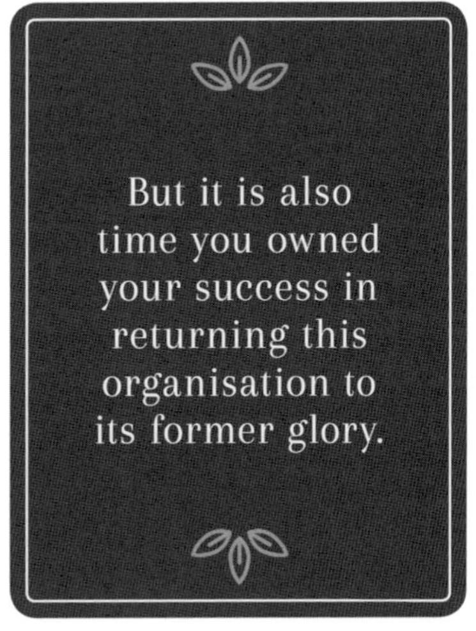
But it is also time you owned your success in returning this organisation to its former glory.

At this dinner, I was seated at the top table beside the executive chairman of a large financial institution based in London. I was shocked when, turning to me, he said, 'I admire the way you have supported the team and allowed them to grow and flourish, but it is also time you owned your success in returning this organisation to its former glory.'

I had fallen into the classic trap of not seeking praise for what I had done because it might be considered I was stepping on others' toes. I was very lucky that the man in question is a very enlightened mentor. His intervention enabled me to claim my due at the right time, in front of some very influential people, and be recognised as the successful leader I was.

Why Is Collaboration Better?

Competition is good but too much can lead to a 'silo mentality' and isolation.

Collaboration is also good. The best balance in leadership provides a place for both, without compromising personal and team integrity. So what are the key concepts that make for good collaboration?

- A silo mentality can stifle creativity and lead to inefficiency. If the working environment has too much focus on individual achievement inefficiency creeps in. When people start believing they need to hold onto information, rather than share it, the result is a fractured team and an inefficient business as the same tasks are being done by several individuals. Sharing information means team members are all focused on aspects of the business or project that are necessary for success.
- Humans are collaborative. This is why it feels more comfortable being the member of a team with a feeling type leadership tool kit. Collaboration is important as a team can be proud of each other's achievements and also see the benefits in working together for a common goal.

- Without collaboration, organisational change will not happen. Women are better at implementing this business strategy. People need to feel connected and involved in what they are doing. Otherwise, they will naturally show resistance.
- Having a shared purpose that focuses on a common goal achieves greater success. Not only do we intrinsically know this, but research into business practice has demonstrated that this is the case time and again. When the whole team buys into the goal, then everyone is working towards the same outcome. When this doesn't happen, members of the team pull in different directions and create disharmony. This can result in failure, as the goal will not be achieved.
- Collaboration promotes diversity of opinion. When a team really feels that not only their opinion is valued but that they will get credit where credit is due, then a real diversity of opinions results. This means it is possible to access additional, first-rate ideas, to assist problem solving and help drive the team forward to achieve success.

It is important to create a careful balance between collaboration and when it is appropriate to accept recognition for success. The next step on the ladder will be considering how to balance all this and also ensure you are looking after yourself.

Key Strategies to Climb the Ladder

- Use your knowledge and understanding of personal preferences and types to ensure you get the right feel for who your team is and how they work together.
- Beware of the boys' club. Aim to be yourself and avoid becoming one of the boys.
- The most successful teams collaborate. Collaboration works better than competition in building successful teams.

Scan this code to get a discount when
you take your Training Styles Indicator
and Hemispheric Indicator Questionnaire.
www.magsinspires.com/4MAT/Bookdiscount

RUNG 7

Looking After Yourself

My promotion to the post of Executive Chairman of an agricultural company in Australia was a real achievement and remains a career highlight, even though I have since accomplished considerably more. The role carried enormous responsibilities.

The nature of the business meant being on call 24 hours a day, seven days a week. The company covered every aspect of farming from food production, through processing and package, to wholesale marketing. There was never any opportunity for rest and relaxation. Plants don't stop growing; wholesale markets traditionally open earlier than retail markets; and produce is best harvested in the early morning and processed during the day to keep it fresh.

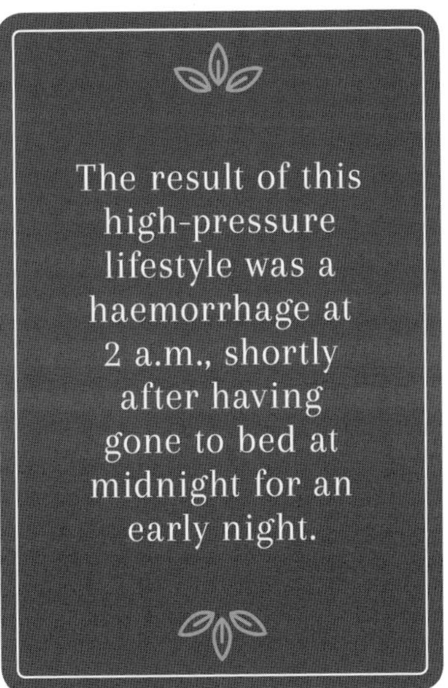
The result of this high-pressure lifestyle was a haemorrhage at 2 a.m., shortly after having gone to bed at midnight for an early night.

We ran four sites in two states. If you are not familiar with Australia, the distance I had to travel between two of the key sites was the same as a trip from Inverness to Plymouth in the UK, or a drive from Los Angeles to the Oregon border in the USA. This was my regular journey. When work finished for the day on one site I left for the other site to be ready for the start of the day there. I often fitted in a visit to the wholesale site on the way. Consequently, I lived my life on the road. My mobile phone was my best friend and my diet was inconsistent. Looking back, I realise I generally had one meal a day around 11 p.m., and inevitably it was junk food!

The result of this high-pressure lifestyle was a haemorrhage at 2 a.m., shortly after having gone to bed at midnight for an early night. I didn't have an ulcer, but I was overweight from lack of exercise and a junk food diet. In a nutshell, my mildly gluten-intolerant body had rebelled. Neglecting my health, especially my diet, had turned my mild intolerance into a full-blown allergy, and ever since I have had the doubtful privilege of visiting hospitals around the world when I have accidentally eaten something containing gluten.

This was a wake-up call for me, and one reason why I chose to step down from this role and take stock of my life.

Women are notorious for putting the health and well-being of others before their own. It is most prevalent amongst those who are climbing the corporate ladder. Caught up in a perceived need to accomplish specific things to demonstrate they are serious about their roles can often damage both their lifestyle and health. Ultimately, the necessity of maintaining a healthy work–life balance, and protecting their mental health is the reason women step off the leadership ladder. They may move successfully into a sphere they were never actually qualified for, and may even set up their own business. It is fantastic when women take on entrepreneurial roles, but a great shame when the need to look after their health and welfare prevents them from taking on roles in male-dominated industries, which, quite frankly, could do with their particular brand of leadership.

Family versus Career

"Being a parent is too complicated and emotional a task for magic techniques and miracle cures."

–Ron Taffel

There is one more huge component in our lives when we try to find a balance between career and lifestyle – whether to have a family or not.

A few years ago, I was talking with a young woman at a leadership conference who asked me how I had managed to choose between career and motherhood. This has stayed in the back of my mind, mainly because I have never made that choice. I have always believed I could have it all. On reflection, I realised that many young women I had worked with had asked me this question in one way or another; but the young men I had worked with had never asked it. Like me, they believed they could have it all. Their assumption, I suspect, was and generally continues to be that someone else will take on the lion's share of the work involved in bringing up a child.

From a young age, I made the decision to have a family and a career. I don't consider these to be mutually exclusive. Sadly, I don't have a family for other reasons totally beyond my control.

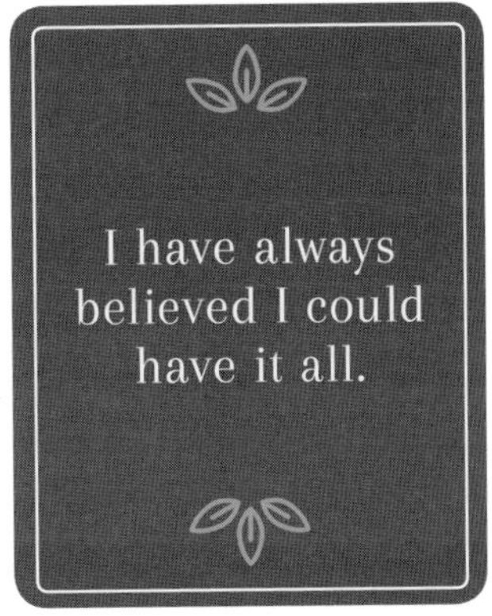
I have always believed I could have it all.

Unfortunately, the majority of women, at some stage in their career, continue to feel they have to make a choice. Of course, a lot of things have changed since I was little. There is better maternity leave and even paternity leave in place. Many countries are beginning to legislate so maternity and paternity leave will have the same options. Laws are in place to ensure women no longer experience discrimination if they choose to have children. More men are opting to be the stay-at-home parents. All this is admirable, but, unfortunately, whilst some areas of society have embraced this, it is not universally recognised.

The stereotypical notion that a woman's place is in the home is still very common. In many societies, young girls are still being put under pressure to behave in a decorous manner and not be too clever for their own good. Teachers who work with secondary-school pupils see this on a daily basis. Too many children are still growing up in an environment where Mum does most of the work at home, whilst Dad focuses on working and paying the bills. Even when Mum is the breadwinner, in both single- and dual-parent families, it is still considered the mother's duty to undertake the childcare role, including delivering and collecting children from school, to taking time off work to look after them.

Ava is a young senior architect. In the five years since her daughter's birth, she has had difficulty finding a balance between parenting and work. For instance, she has to drop her daughter at school on the way to work, and so reaches her office after nine. She also has to leave work if there is any problem with her daughter during the school day. Ava's husband runs his own business and sets his own hours. There is absolutely no reason why he cannot do both these tasks, but he finds plausible reasons, such as meetings, to avoid doing so.

Interestingly, many women choose to run their own businesses so they can have the flexibility to do the very things Ava's husband will not take responsibility for.

Mary, another working mother, has been really fortunate to work in a company that is flexible and willing to accommodate her childcare needs, but this means she has to spend weekends at work making up time on projects.

As we get older and go to work, prejudices continue in the workplace. Although it is illegal, women are still being discriminated against in many workplaces because they have children. Whilst this isn't immediately obvious, it exists and is commonly seen when mothers cannot consistently fulfil the number of working hours expected because of childcare commitments. This is seen as a lack of dedication to their career, even if they complete all the tasks their role demands. I know there are companies that are supportive of men and women balancing their careers with family life, but unfortunately they are very much the minority.

Diane, who works in a large government organisation, has recently been overlooked for promotion because of her pregnancy and this happened at the end of 2015! Although it is difficult to prove, several things happened that support the suggestion this was the reason. A 'well meaning' senior leader suggested they would understand if she chose not to go for a position she was fully qualified for because of all she was currently dealing with. As well as being in her last months of pregnancy a close relative had died when she was applying for the promotion.

This might seem to have been genuine concern for Diane's situation, but when we look beneath the surface, other discriminatory factors were involved. She had been undertaking the role she was applying for on a time-share basis with the head of the department, who had recently retired, and for three months had held the position, whilst the recruitment process swung into gear. She was also recognised by other government bodies for her competence and achievements in this role. Nevertheless, she wasn't offered the post. The individual who was awarded the role didn't have as much experience, but **he** was not pregnant and about to take maternity leave.

It is this type of action that explains why so many young women still think they need to make a choice. How do we change this?

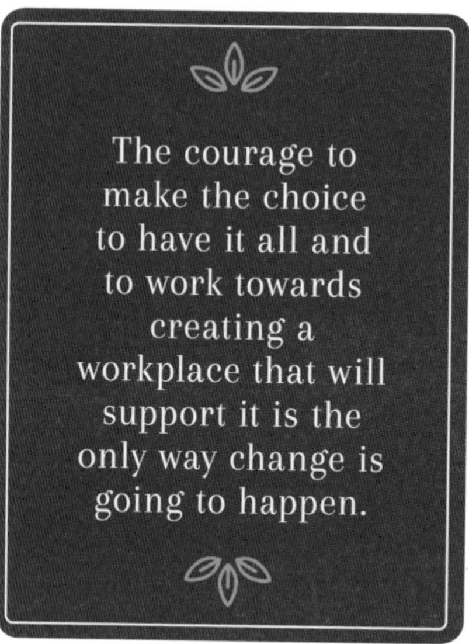
The courage to make the choice to have it all and to work towards creating a workplace that will support it is the only way change is going to happen.

Not all organisations behave in this way, and it doesn't occur in all countries as some cultures are far more enlightened. In countries like the UK, the USA and Australia, even though there are options in place to put men into roles, they are not necessarily being taken up. Men also have to deal with prejudice in some situations. Other countries are a little more accepting culturally both generally and within organisations.

Solveig is married with two children and lives in Denmark. Just before she knew she was expecting her second child, Solveig was headhunted for a new role. She is in charge of the strategy and branding for the whole company. It is a new initiative for the organization. Initially, like any new person, regardless of sex, especially taking up a role that involves change, she had to deal with the 'who are you to come in and implement this?' attitude from others in the company.

She had originally been employed to cover a maternity leave contract and now was faced with explaining she was pregnant herself! The company was both understanding and helpful. Instead of getting upset at this unexpected turn of events, they offered her a permanent position instead of a contract to ensure they would keep her.

We need more organisations around the world like that!

Changing organisational culture is not going to happen overnight. Rather, it is something that will only come about when more people make the change from within. The courage to make the choice to have it all and to work towards creating a workplace that will support it is the only way change is going to happen. Having the courage to approach your employers and persuade them to value you as Solveig managed to do in just four months, will do more to bring this about. Simply saying it should happen won't alter anything. When your record speaks for itself, they will not only promote you but will also recognise that pregnancy is no bar to this and will support your wish to have a family.

Exercise: Visualisation

Imagine the future when you have a young family. What does this look like? Who picks the children up from school? Who makes their meals? Who cleans up the house? Go through all the activities that would be involved in having a family.

Record them in the space provide below or in your notebook.

____

____

____

____

Now I want you to visualise how this equates with your career plans, or your current role if you are already in leadership. How does your picture of family life fit in with your current work role? Will it work, or can you see difficulties managing this? Who do you visualise as being responsible for the children before and after school? Did you automatically assume it would be you? If so, why? Are you stereotyping yourself? What are the barriers you see? How do you envisage overcoming them?

Record your thoughts in the space below or in your notebook.

____

____

____

____

Now consider how you could make the two work together. What would have to be put in place? What might have to change? To help you 'have it all' you now have a goal.

Long Hours

Another barrier is late-night socialising, or after-hours work that is built into corporate culture. This is a very male model of doing business. Whether they have a young family or not, many women don't feel happy with this work-based socialising. Nowadays, many men aren't keen on it either. It seems to be a cultural hangover connected with the competitive model of climbing the ladder. If you aren't seen to be working late you can't be committed and loyal to your company.

It might be considered amusing that this culture continues to exist in a lot of companies, when numerous studies have shown productivity and creativity are actually reduced, but it isn't. So how do you deal with it if you are in this type of work environment?

First, you should prioritise your workload so the evidence of what you contribute can be seen, whilst demonstrating nothing is gained by working such long hours. This is not an easy task. When I worked at the agricultural company, my hours were ridiculously long. I could be in one site office at 5 a.m. running a 'tool box' meeting with staff. I would then spend the rest of the day, until 10 or 11 at night, dealing with various issues, before moving on to the next site to deal with employee issues until after midnight. Unbelievably, I would then drive to my motel where I would snatch about three hours sleep before leaving, just after 6 a.m., to reach the next site by 9 a.m. to deal with all their issues.

Crazy!

My role as group HR manager was very new, and the company owner had little idea of what it involved. As well as constantly travelling between all the company sites, I was also expected to attend arbitration meetings and to sit on various committees.

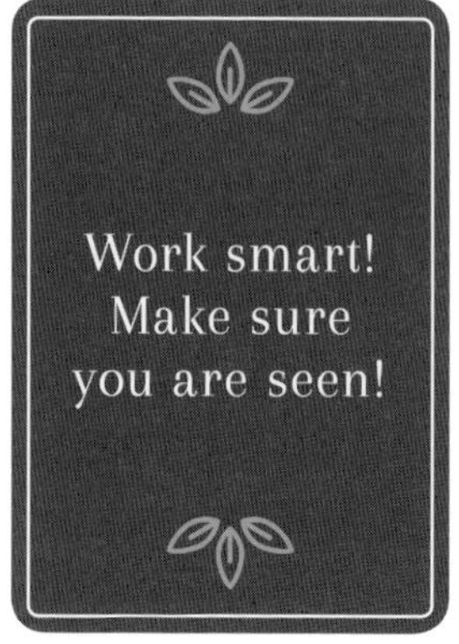
Work smart!
Make sure
you are seen!

Consequently, large amounts of my time were spent out of the office. The owner was used to dealing with people he saw every day because they only worked on one site. The other managers worked from 6 a.m. to 4 p.m. or 8 a.m. to 5 p.m., and so he could see they were all busy. The problem for me was that, whilst I was working much longer hours on many sites, I was out of sight and so out of mind!

As you will remember from earlier, this affected me adversely. My key point is that if you want to make progress up the ladder, you must organise your work life intelligently. Work smart! Make sure you are seen!

Exercise: Work-Life Balance

To help you recognise how work impacts your life, complete the following tables or copy them into your notebook. Do this activity quickly rather than spending time thinking about your answers. It requires your gut reaction.

1. Give yourself a grade from 1 to 5 in each area, where 1 means you are doing well and 5 means you are not doing it at all, or you are doing it really badly.
2. List the key opportunity or problem that needs to be resolved in that area.
3. List the first action you need to take to capitalise on the opportunity or start to solve the problem.

Area	Grade	Opportunity/Problem	Action to take
Physical Exercise			
Eating Habits			
Drinking, smoking			
Mental Health			
Spiritual (personal time out)			
Relationships – Business Contacts			
Relationships – Personal			
Financial Health			
Work Hours			
Family Time			

Now you should have a clearer picture of what needs to be done so you are 'working smarter', but still in a way that ensures you are recognised for the contribution you make, as well as balancing it with your personal needs.

Balancing career ambitions, family and work hours can require a lot of juggling and it is important to stay on top of it, unless you want to end up, as I did, using hindsight to achieve a more balanced life. It is also important to look after your mental health, which can easily be affected by the factors you have been considering.

Key Strategies to Climb the Ladder:

- Career and family are possible. Men have been doing it for thousands of years. You can too!
- Take care of your health, nobody else will, and if you don't, you cannot successfully climb the ladder.
- Long hours don't get you noticed. You may have to do some occasionally, but generally you need to work smarter.

RUNG 8

Mental Health

"Mental illness is an equal opportunity illness. Every one of us is impacted by mental illness. One in five adults is dealing with this illness, and many are not seeking help because the stigma prevents that."

—Margaret Larson

Mental health is important. It is also the hidden 'disease'. Unfortunately, I have been bullied in two companies I have worked for. Regrettably, this isn't as uncommon as you might hope. It is also frequently experienced by high-achieving women who are climbing, or could potentially climb, the leadership ladder. Bullying is never a good thing, often leading to depression and anxiety in victims.

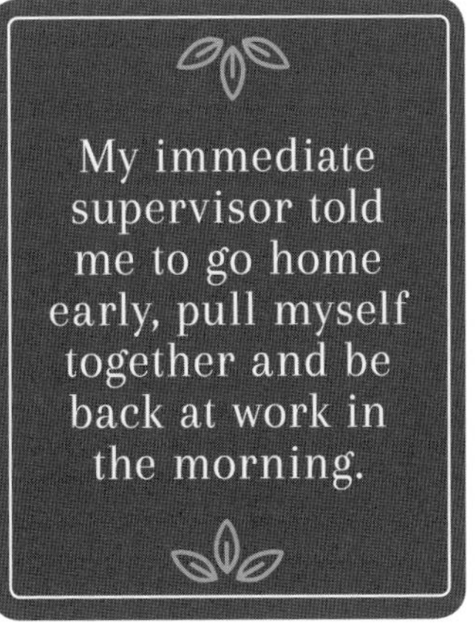
My immediate supervisor told me to go home early, pull myself together and be back at work in the morning.

The potential for depression and anxiety is multiplied for me as I am bipolar. Bipolar disorder is not curable. Many highly successful people have revealed they are sufferers, often only after they have achieved success. Stephen Fry is one high-profile example.

I am no different in admitting to this, but it isn't always easy to do so. No sufferer should have to lie, but unfortunately if you aren't a celebrity you may feel it is not a good idea to admit to suffering from it because mental illness is still stigmatised.

In one post I held, I broke down one day and ended up crying in front of everyone. I couldn't stop! This wasn't the first manifestation of the 'problem'. Long before I broke down, I was coming to work exhausted because I was waking up in the middle of the night crying. If your work position is affecting your health to this extent, regardless of your personal health background, do something about changing it. My immediate supervisor told me to go home early – it was actually normal knock-off time, but I generally worked on for an average of four hours. I was told to 'pull myself together and be back at work in the morning'. I had already informed my employers I was seeking medical advice, but had been ignored. This time my extreme trauma had been caused by working unsupported with 20 high-need, traumatised individuals. My repeated requests for support had been ignored.

Eventually, I made the decision to leave, particularly as the role wasn't in my career plan; even though it was something I used to enjoy doing. The effect on me was huge, although any individual suffering from work-induced anxiety would have had similar symptoms. It triggered a major depressive cycle. These don't happen often for me, I am what is known as a *cyclothymic*. This means I have periods of hypomania, periods of normalcy and sometimes mild depression in between. It was depression that originally led me to seek help. I had my first episode at 17, and my next major one aged 32. However, I would be the first to admit I like the hypomanic periods because I get so much done.

Mental Health Is Not Something to 'Get Over'

Bipolar disorder is generally seen as a major incurable mental health issue, and sufferers frequently face discrimination. Anxiety and depression are also chronic disorders that don't simply disappear if you take a tablet or go home early. People with these disorders include teachers, lawyers, doctors, nurses, actors, janitors, CEOs and many, many more professionals. Their mental health problems are no hindrance to succeeding in their roles, or even climbing their career ladder. A general lack of understanding, not only amongst employers but amongst the general public, is the reason why people feel they have to hide their condition.

If you want to succeed, it doesn't matter if you have an underlying, long-term mental problem, experience depression, anxiety, or both on a short-term basis, or suffer from something that is an inherent part of you, as bipolar disorder is for me, you need to take care of your mental health. It is as important as caring for your physical health.

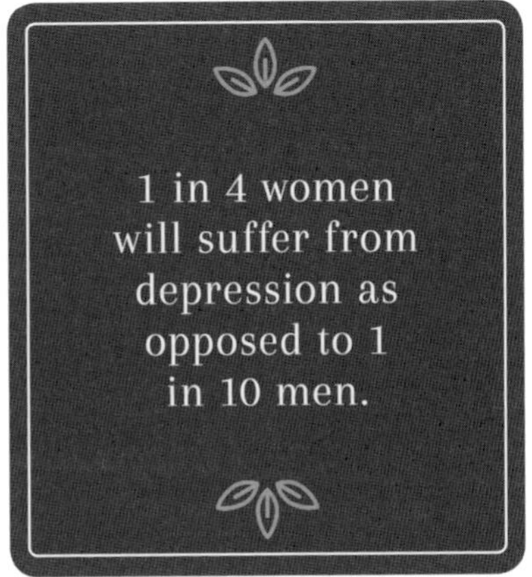
1 in 4 women
will suffer from
depression as
opposed to 1
in 10 men.

In our effort to become superwomen we often forget this.

In the United Kingdom, according to the National Health Service, 1 in 4 women will suffer from depression as opposed to 1 in 10 men. In the UK, 29% of women report a major mental health issue compared to 17% of men. This is thought to be because women will talk about it more freely. Women are twice as likely as men to experience some kind of anxiety disorder. According to the Australian Bureau of Statistics, 22% of women are likely to experience a mental health issue for 12 months or more compared to 17% of men. In the United States, a study reported in *Time*

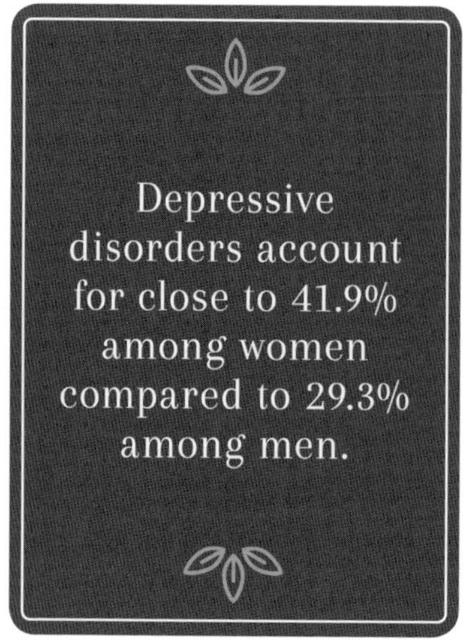
Depressive disorders account for close to 41.9% among women compared to 29.3% among men.

Magazine showed 9% of women and 5% of men had experienced depression in the previous 12 months, with 23% of women suffering from an anxiety disorder compared with 14% of men.

A World Health Organization report also shows women are more likely to be affected by mental health issues. The latest statistics, as summarised in a report for the 2013 to 2020 Mental Health Action Plan, are:

- Depressive disorders account for close to 41.9% of disability from neuropsychiatric disorders among women compared to 29.3% among men.
- Leading mental health problems in older adults are depression, organic brain syndromes and dementia – the majority of sufferers are women.
- An estimated 80% of 50 million people affected by violent conflicts, civil wars, disasters and displacement are women and children.
- Lifetime prevalence rate of violence against women ranges from 16% to 50%.
- At least one in five women suffers rape or attempted rape in their lifetime.

These statistics are alarming, especially when mental health is persistently not taken seriously. There is still a real stigma attached to it, and any history of anxiety or depression is one of the most common barriers to leadership. This is an issue for both men and women.

When you suffer from 'less curable' mental health issues it is even harder as you are often forced to hide them. This raises even more issues and puts a strain on your health. Good mental health is important, but it is frequently overlooked.

A general perception persists that if you have any type of mental illness you are somehow less capable of working; not just in leadership roles, but in general this is not the case. There are many highly successful people with mental health issues who have successful careers and have been successful leaders. These include Oprah Winfrey, who has an anxiety disorder; JP Morgan, who is bipolar; Robin Williams, who suffered from clinical depression; and Marsha Lineman, who has borderline personality disorder. These are some of the well-known people who have bravely admitted to having mental problems, but there are so many more that prefer to hide their problems.

Whatever anybody may think, those with mental health issues are no more likely to have problems at work than those with physical problems, or none. For example, being a leader with mental issues doesn't mean they will become a tyrannical leader – that is the realm of psychopaths, not the clinically depressed.

Leadership and Mental Health

Whether you are a leader who at some stage may suffer from mental health issues, or one who is lucky enough to be in the 75% of the population who aren't affected, it is important to create an environment friendly towards those who may be dealing with mental health issues regardless of whether these are short or long term.

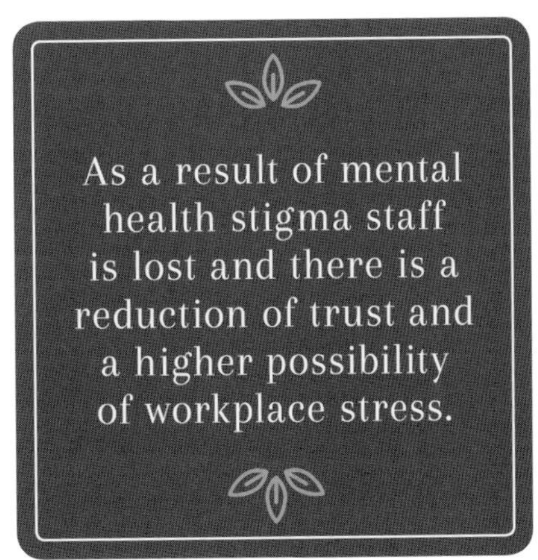
As a result of mental health stigma staff is lost and there is a reduction of trust and a higher possibility of workplace stress.

One of the biggest workplace problems is stress. This can be caused by working conditions, how people treat you, or even your own perceptions of what you should be doing. Research about the effects of workplace stress conducted by Mind, a UK-based charity, revealed that:

- More than 1 in 5 (21%) agreed that they had called in sick to avoid work.
- Fourteen percent agreed that they had resigned and 42% had considered resigning.
- Thirty percent of staff disagreed with the statement 'I would feel able to talk openly with my line manager if I was feeling stressed.'
- Fifty-six percent of employers said they would like to do more to improve staff wellbeing but didn't feel they had received the right training or guidance.

Mental health has a major impact on the workplace whether we like it or not. As a result of mental health stigma staff is lost and there is a reduction of trust and a higher possibility of workplace stress. Whilst mental health is now talked about and at last even governments are trying to make a difference, it is going to take a much greater effort to eliminate this stigma. In 2016 the UK Government introduced a programme called 'Time to Change'; unfortunately, it only focuses on a small aspect of what needs to be done if openness and awareness are to be recognised and understood in the workplace.

As a leader you have a responsibility to create an environment where people feel comfortable and are happy to speak to you about their issues. This can be difficult in an environment where so little is understood about mental illness and how it can and does affect our ability to communicate and work.

My cyclothymic bipolar disorder does not affect my day-to-day ability to work. Actually, a lot of the time it has enabled me to achieve some good things rather than spoiling them. Even in my depressive episodes I have been able to achieve. Unfortunately, because of the actions of one person when, at the age of 17, I revealed my problem, I subsequently decided it was better to keep such information to myself. Thus, when I suffered from a depressive episode at the age of 32, I kept it to myself and worked on.

At 17, I opened up and told teachers at my school what was happening to me. Most were sympathetic, supportive and eager to do what they could to help. Unfortunately, one was less sympathetic, and, breaching confidentially, relayed something I had told them in confidence to other students. As if this was not enough he took it upon himself to inform everyone I was blaming staff for my problems and was crazy! This was extremely unprofessional and left me feeling I was to blame for revealing how I felt. Possibly because of his attitude, which might well have affected my ambition, I worked extremely hard and was awarded the Science Dux without the help of my unsupportive chemistry teacher.

By the time I was 32, times had changed a little, but as I was working in an all-male environment and had just been appointed chairman of the board, I felt this was not the time to reveal anything that might indicate I was weak in any way. So not only did I deal with this privately, only revealing my depression to close family, but I managed to keep my position within the organisation.

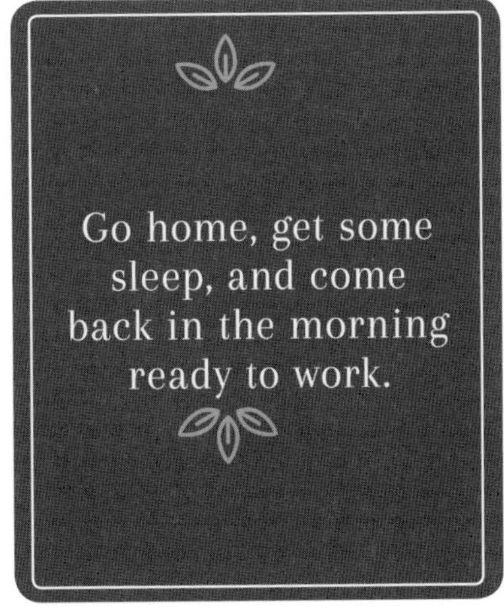
Go home, get some sleep, and come back in the morning ready to work.

None of what I have revealed is to suggest I am amazing; rather it is to highlight the need for support and understanding. As a leader with a mental health diagnosis that I deal with on a daily basis, I am more attuned to the need to be open and approachable, which must have communicated itself to others in the way I operate, as I have always been the recipient of my team's confidences.

Sadly, over the years I have seen far too many leaders who consider the 'go home and get over' mantra is appropriate, and so I particularly remember that supervisor who told me to 'go home, get some sleep, and come back in the morning ready to work'.

Taking Care of Your Mental Health

As both leader and individual you owe it to yourself to look after your greatest asset – your health, both mental and physical. You would go to the doctor if you had the flu or some other physical illness, and, in the same way, you need to make sure you receive the right advice and attention when there are problems with your mental health.

Many people can be cured. Just as we will suffer from a physical complaint at times, many of us will suffer from depression, stress-related illnesses or anxiety, which will be brought on by a particular set of circumstances. Often, once these circumstances are removed, dealt with in some other way or a sufficient amount of time has elapsed since they occurred, we will recover, but this is no reason to hang in there hoping it will be the case.

When the problem is an inherent part of who you are, it also needs to be looked after. We need to ensure we have counselling if this works; take the pills that reduce the intensity of an anxiety attack; or look at our current situation and find ways to cope with it so we can continue working. This is not about giving up dreams; this is about looking after yourself so you can experience the maximum success possible.

Key steps you can take to ensure your mental health:

- Talk about your feelings. This does not mean talking to all and sundry about them. Talk to people you trust and who will understand your needs, but not necessarily feel the need to 'fix you'.
- Keep active. Whilst this is difficult, particularly when you are crippled with an anxiety attack or in the midst of a depressive episode, it is a good habit to maintain. It really does help your mental health to be active.
- Ask for help. If you are feeling overwhelmed in some way, or even if it has not yet reached this stage, it is sensible to ask for help.
- Don't forget to take time for yourself. Take a break. It could be reading a book or watching your favourite TV show without feeling guilty. It could be a spa day, a short break or holiday or walking in the hills. Whatever it is you do to relax, remember to timetable it into your life, especially when you are busy.

Exercise: Personal Time Inventory

Often we don't actually realise how we are spending our time, which means that when it comes to addressing our personal health, it may be too late. The following exercise is designed to help you review what you are doing in an average week. Whilst it is generally used to help you recognise how much time you are wasting, it is a great tool for seeing if you are getting enough 'me' time during your week.

For a more accurate estimate of your week, keep track of how you spend your time. Carry a weekly calendar with you, and document your activities throughout the day. You can then complete this survey with the calendar to refer to.

How are using your time?

Hours spent sleeping per night: ______x 7 = ______
Hours spent preparing meals and eating: ______x 7 = ______
Hours per day spent grooming: ______x 7 = ______
Hours spent exercising: ______x 7 = ______
(Include travel/extra grooming time)

Hours spent at work (or in classes) per week: = ______
Total travel time, week days: = ______

Hours per week for regularly scheduled functions: = ______
(Clubs, meetings, study group, religious meetings, other...)

Hours per day doing errands, cleaning, checking on the progress of tasks delegated to others: ______x 7 = ______

Hours per day spent socialising: ______x 7 = ______

Understanding your mental health and what you need to do to maintain it is not just something you need to do for you on an individual level but it is also something that you need to be aware of as a leader. Be open to talking about it and also being there for others to talk to in a supportive and non-judgemental way is imperative. It is also important for you to have people to talk to from a personal and career perspective.

Key Strategies to Climb the Ladder

- Understand the impact of mental health on the workplace and that it is not something that is a barrier to work.
- Make sure you put strategies in place as a leader to allow others to feel comfortable talking about mental health.
- Ensure you take care of your own mental health as a leader and an individual as it is as important as your physical health to personal success.

Scan this code for more information
on workplace wellness audits, personal
wellness audits and training programs
on wellness that are offered by Maggie.
www.magsinspires.com/Wellness

RUNG 9

Mentor or Coach? That Is the Question

"Your decisions, not your conditions, determine your destiny."

—Mary Cantando

Many people ask whether it is better to have a mentor or a coach, and the reasons for choosing either are often misunderstood, so I want to share a little story with you.

I have already mentioned that my first step on the leadership ladder was my role with the large agricultural company in Australia. I was employed as the personnel and training officer. This role, as the title suggests, was a lower-level human resources job and, as an engineer, I was taking a step away from production. It was technically a step down from the production management role I had held in my previous company, but I was looking for a change in direction

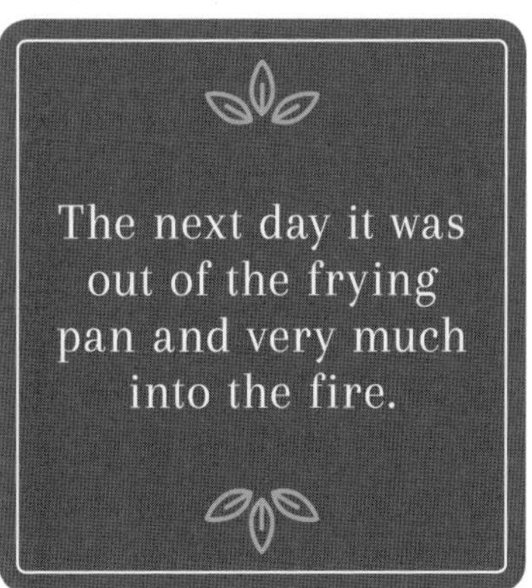
The next day it was out of the frying pan and very much into the fire.

and training and development was an area I really wanted to pursue. It was also a step into a much larger company, as I finally made the move from a small and medium enterprise.

On my first day, I found the amount of work that needed to be done to bring this company up to speed really stimulating. The role was just what I wanted in order to further my career. The operations manager was also in charge of human resources. I spent most of my first day working with him to find out what had and what hadn't been done. It didn't take me long to realise he wasn't somebody I could work with, or who would be prepared to show me the ropes. At the time, he was holding down two senior leadership roles, and to be honest, the human resource role was the poor relation. Nevertheless, I realised I could still learn from him and was up to the task.

The next day it was out of the frying pan and very much into the fire. My first task was to assist the wholesale site manager with a dismissal. This should have been straightforward, but the information in the file that should have explained the situation was minimal. Making sure I left our head office site by 5 p.m. to get some rest, I headed to our market site for an 11 p.m. meeting with the manager, from whom I hoped to elicit the relevant information.

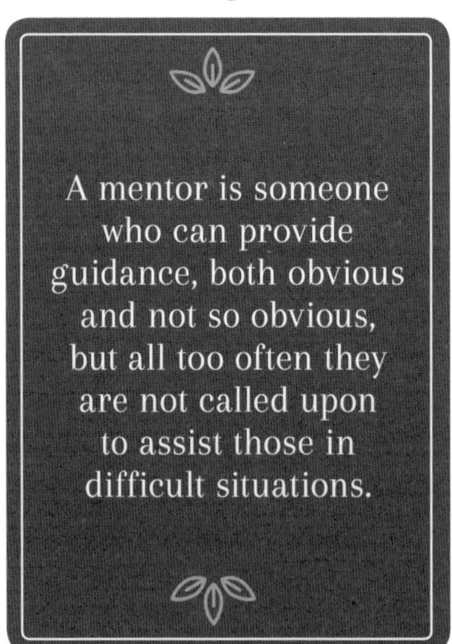
A mentor is someone who can provide guidance, both obvious and not so obvious, but all too often they are not called upon to assist those in difficult situations.

It turned out to be far more difficult than I had envisaged. The manager wanted to dismiss a woman because she had been missing work about once a week. I explained that without official warnings this was not possible. Next, I had a one-to-one conversation with her, where she revealed her absence from work coincided with inappropriate advances made by the manager. This sexual harassment case, in the 98%-male-dominated workforce, was being totally ignored.

I tell this story because, with no experience to draw on, it was my task to deal with the situation; one that, unfortunately, is still a frequent occurrence in many industries. In this situation, having a mentor to advise me would have been really helpful.

Mentoring as a Means of Learning and Growing

A mentor is someone who can provide guidance, both obvious and not so obvious, but all too often they are not called upon to assist those in difficult situations. Frequently they are individuals we are not aware of. They are people who feel drawn to help us develop, provide support and challenge us to help this happen. I really could have done with one when faced with my first sexual harassment case.

There are many mentoring programmes available for both men and women who want to make progress in their careers. Some specifically for women, such as the Cherie Blair Foundation, have successful men and women volunteers mentoring women in, or starting out in, business. These programmes are fantastic and provide a good source of expertise to draw on. What must be emphasised is that a mentor is not someone you make formal arrangements with, and so you may be totally unaware they are available for you to consult. Often, they are people you work with whom you didn't even realise were mentoring you. You need to keep your eyes open so you can recognise them and ask for support when you need it.

Looking back to that first harassment situation, with nobody within the company to turn to for advice and expertise, I now realise there were some great mentors around, but they weren't working in my company. Since then, over the years, I have joined several organisations to help me with personal growth and further my development as a leader. This is where I found my mentors. That is now, but at the time I felt I was totally on my own.

Whilst I would encourage you to actively seek and work with someone who can mentor you, it is even more important that you don't discount the network you are working with.

On reflection, during that period of time when I thought I was on my own, just after that first sexual harassment case I had to deal with, I wasn't. I had a great mentor in the company's lawyer. He was always challenging and stretching me, getting me to play to my strengths, and he balanced this with sage advice and encouragement that really helped me stretch my wings. At the time, I did not directly see this for what it was.

Many of you are probably only now realising how many mentors you really have or have had so far in your career.

As I moved on to higher level roles in the company, there were more people mentoring me, although I didn't realise it until years later. It was only when I started doing the same for young men and women that I realised just what these people had done for me.

Exercise: Who Are My Mentors?

Here is an exercise that should get you thinking about your mentors. Take a few minutes to write a list of everyone you have worked with or are connected to who may have been offering you advice or challenging your thought processes to test and stretch you. You can use the space below or enter their names in your notebook:

____

____

____

Coaching: A Tool to Help You Get the Best out of Yourself

The clear distinction between a mentor and a coach needs to be made at this juncture. A mentor, whether they are someone we have sought out or someone who is doing it informally, offers advice when needed, and not always when it is asked for! They also offer support when it is required, and challenge us in ways which at times can be really uncomfortable. Sometimes they tell us what could be the right way to proceed, but usually they guide and help us to find our own pathways.

A coach is similar, but you have a formal and acknowledged relationship with them, and they are usually paid. Their primary role is to push you, challenge you, help you to find your own path and bring out the best in you. A coach may or may not be an expert in the area you work in or are aiming for. Their expertise lies in helping people recognise what they need to do to move forward.

A coach is someone to work with in partnership, to help reach a goal or overcome an obstacle. They are there to encourage you to explore what needs to be done. They ask questions to make you think about a process and, through their understanding and insight, know what buttons they need to push to help you decide. A coach is a good person to have whenever you are looking to move forward, change direction or just grow within your current role.

As they are there to help you make independent decisions, it is better if your coach isn't a friend, although they can be someone you admire. They are also not connected with your work. They can be trusted completely with the information you share, and you will often need to share things that are very personal in order to make progress in your chosen role.

It is really important to be open to the questions your coach may ask, no matter how challenging they may seem, but most of all you need to be willing to work with them. As with a mentor, there is no magic pill or solution. They are there to provide guidance, whilst leaving implementation to you.

An Aside – Now to Continue My Story

I was in a very painful situation and it stretched me incredibly. Inevitably, I made mistakes, but I finally managed to stumble my way to a successful conclusion. The manager in question was, after a thorough investigation, disciplined and finally dismissed. I also learned a valuable lesson when the young lady, who was at the start of her career, kept her job but eventually left. Unfortunately, because it had taken far too long to resolve the case, she felt she was working in an environment where the support she needed had been too little too late. As a result, she was not comfortable working with the company any more, even though the manager had been dismissed. She did, however, continue to follow her chosen career path, finding another company to work for where there was no underlying resentment.

I did find two mentors, although at the time I was not aware they were available. They helped me grow, not only in my role as personnel and training officer but also eventually as the human resource manager, as I had demonstrated my competency to my employers in such a short space of time. I might possibly have climbed the ladder without my mentors' support, but I would not have progressed nearly so quickly. If I hadn't made the effort, not only to develop my knowledge of the role's requirements but also to educate both staff and management in the company, it might never have happened. Such actions are a very important aspect of leadership.

Leader as a Trainer

"Your 'enemies' are your greatest teachers. Be grateful for them and they will lose their power over you."

—CJ Scarlet

So far, we have looked at developing our leadership skills, now I want to look at why it is important to help others develop theirs. The greatest attribute of a leader is understanding that those they guide will eventually move on, and that is their goal.

It is important to know yourself; how you like to learn and, consequently, how you like to train others. This affects how you communicate with them.

I tend to be a blue-sky thinker. I like to look at the big picture and ultimately trust someone will be there to fill in the details so I can make things happen. I have always included at least one person in my team who prefers to work with detail, to ensure this is possible. I have never really thought about the impact my preferred style of leadership may have on these members of my team until now.

My style of leadership works well if the person prefers to work with detail and also asks a lot of questions. I often find this frustrating, but at least I am made aware of their need for more information. I had one particular human resources assistant shortly after I took on this role. I had carefully selected a graduate with the intention of training them up.

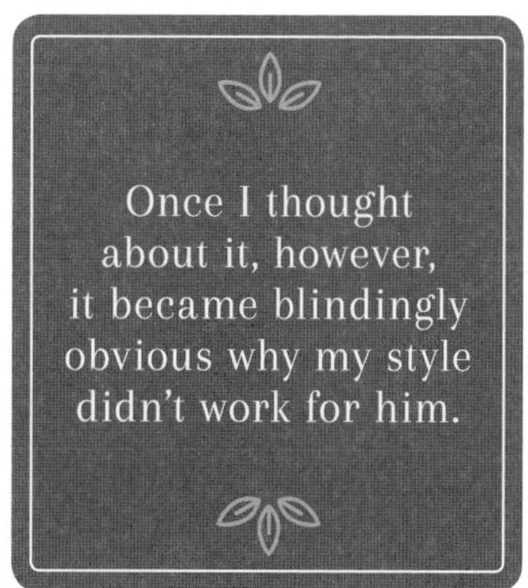
Once I thought
about it, however,
it became blindingly
obvious why my style
didn't work for him.

I really liked their attention to detail as it meant I could leave much of that type of work to them. I was excited about working with and developing someone so early in their career, who had so much potential.

I failed miserably.

At the time, I couldn't understand why. I was just frustrated because he didn't seem to understand what I wanted from him or grasp what I was trying to teach him. I failed to recognise how my preferred method of working and training people was totally at odds with the way this young man preferred to work, whilst he didn't understand or connect with the way I delivered information, and was consequently equally frustrated and confused. To make matters worse, he left thinking I was a poor leader. It isn't surprising that some people will dislike their leaders, but in this case, I was upset with myself for not recognising there was a problem.

Once I thought about it, however, it became blindingly obvious why my style didn't work for him, and this made a huge difference to the way I work now. My preference continues to be getting in there and trying things out, but if this doesn't work I now review my actions and try again. If this works but I think things could still be improved I tinker with it until this is the case. This is why I tend to give those I am responsible for training a little bit of information, and expect them to go off and get on with what I want done.

However, for people who need to build on what they have done before, or require a step-by-step break down on how to do something, and also need to understand why this is the best way, my natural style becomes their worst nightmare!

Once I recognised where I had gone wrong, I understood how important it is for leaders to recognise they are responsible for ensuring all members of their team understand what is expected of them, and what they need to do. Leaders are often responsible for ensuring training is provided so those working for them can perform effectively. Training may be formal and done away from the job, or personnel can be trained on the job by someone else, even you.

Even when you are not actually training a member of your team, you will discover by the very nature of how you work, that you are actually teaching those around you new things, and also training others to perform effectively at the same time. This ensures your team works at its optimum level. You cannot do this effectively if you don't understand how you learn. Once you know, however, your communication with your team will be enhanced.

Your Learning Style

It is a very good idea to determine your learning style, and I wholeheartedly recommend doing so. Here is a simple exercise to give you some guidance, but it is not a substitute for carrying out a proper profile, which will provide you with proper feedback. It isn't possible to offer the full feedback needed in the pages of a book, but the exercise should set you on the right path. Nine phrases are listed below. You need to rank each set of phrases, with four being what **best** characterises your learning style, down to one as least characteristic. Be sure to assign **a different number** to each of the four phrases in each set.

1		I like to analyse		I hesitate		I decide quickly		I am practical
2		I like to listen		I look for something relevant		I like to analyse the information		I tend to postpone decisions
3		I like to relate to real life		I like to listen to new facts		I like to evaluated the information received		I like to apply information in action
4		I normally accept new facts		I like to challenge information		I like to evaluate before accepting		I like to apply information to real life
5		I believe in my intuition		I like concrete facts		I think logically		I like to question
6		I like abstract concepts		I like to observe before acting		I like concrete facts		I like to act immediately
7		I apply facts to present situations		I think about new information		I can relate facts to future situations		I need concrete facts and proof
8		I related new facts to what I already know		I like to observe		I like to turn new facts into new theories		I like to test and see how it works
9		I live with intensity		I am reserved		I think rationally		I do things when I am sure they will work

Now add the values you have given for each of the columns

Concrete:	Reflective:	Theorist:	Active:

Here is a very brief explanation of the type of learner you are and what this means if you are a leader.

Concrete learners perceive information concretely and process it reflectively. They use personal experience to connect and understand why things are happening.

Imaginative thinkers believe in their own experience and excel at looking at experiences from many different perspectives; as learners they need time to process information.

Reflective learners understand information abstractly and process it reflectively. They form theories and concepts by matching observations with known information and value sequential thinking. They need details so they can evaluate information and collect detail. They need assurance.

Theorists understand information abstractly but process it actively. They are hands-on people, who learn by doing and applying common sense to a situation. They like to problem solve and will often resent being given the answers.

Active learners understand what they are told concretely and process it actively. They integrate experience by applying it to something. They learn best by trial and error and love self-discovery. They will often appear to reach a conclusion without being able explain how they got there.

At a very basic level it should now be much clearer how we learn and process information. This can have a profound effect on how we pass information on to others. This is important to know, when expanding our careers. Knowing how we help others learn and grow is a very useful tool to have when climbing the career ladder.

Key Strategies for Climbing the Ladder

- Not all mentors are people you choose, and often they are not immediately obvious. They are great people to have around, not only to help you see the way forward but also to persuade you to tackle situations outside your comfort zone.
- Having a coach is an excellent way of helping you stay on track and set goals in order to advance your career.
- Knowing how you learn and like to teach others is an important tool if you are to make progress in your career.

"A mentor is someone who sees more talent and ability within you, than you see in yourself, and helps bring it out of you."

-Bob Proctor

RUNG 10

Which Ladder Is the Best Ladder for You?

Climbing up the ladder is an exciting journey, but sometimes when we reach the top it is hard to see what is below. We need to be careful when we are climbing to ensure we are on the right ladder and have the right plan in place to make it all happen.

Strategy Is Essential

"Tactics are temporary... Strategy lasts forever!"

–Joy Cook

In one of my first leadership roles I lost my job because I missed the subtle byplay within the business and so failed to use appropriate strategies. I was assistant production manager for a medium-sized agricultural company in Australia's rural Victoria. Although I failed on a strategic level, I have to admit I was entertained by my direct boss who slept at his desk for most of the day. The reason

I lost my job was apparently because I had gone out with the ex-boyfriend of my boss's daughter. They actually ensured that all the systems they wanted set up were in place before they dropped the bombshell. It was certainly quite dramatic, and I left with some wonderful tales to tell in the future. Most importantly, it gave me a much stronger understanding of what to be aware of in the future.

Not all organisations are like *Days of Our Lives*, so it doesn't need to be this obvious.

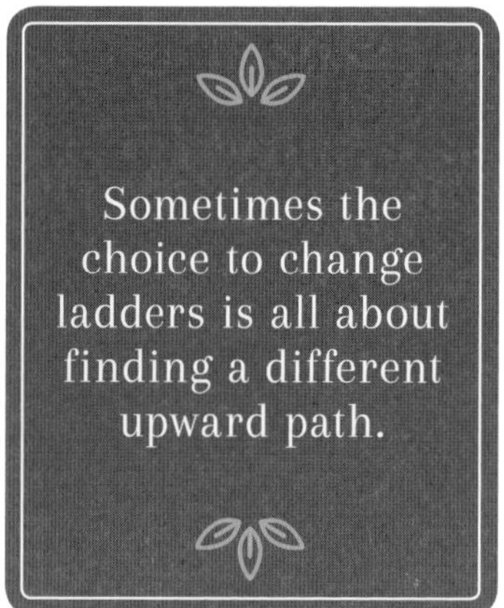

Sometimes the choice to change ladders is all about finding a different upward path.

If I had understood what I was required to do before I embarked on this stage of my career I would have had a much smoother climb up the ladder. It is always important to be prepared to deal with any eventualities beforehand, but even if I had done my homework, I would never have factored in avoiding going out with someone I didn't know with a past connection to the business!

Whether you are building the business or building a career, strategy is essential. Having a strategy is an area many leaders, both male and female, fail to employ. It is often viewed as something to steer clear of as only a certain type of person can behave strategically. I have to admit, strategy is one of my strengths, but this doesn't mean I get things right all the time, and I don't always recognise how I should be applying it to myself.

Early in my career, my inability to recognise I needed to be strategic slowed my progress up the ladder, and I am generally someone who plays to their strengths! If strategy is not a strength, this is an area you really need to develop. If strategy is a strength then you really need to apply strategies in your working environment.

The saying that 'decisions are generally made before you sit down at the boardroom table' is very well known. It is often claimed that they are discussed and decided upon in the men's room; frankly not a domain women can enter, or would want to.

I was sitting at the head of the boardroom table as executive chairman of the board and feeling quite proud that I had achieved this. At the end of my first meeting I realised we had to start implementing a few strategic moves. During this meeting, my fellow board members had decided it would be a good idea to wander in and out, and for one of them not to show up at all. I promise not all board members are like this, but using an extreme case as an example can sometimes help paint a picture of what we often have to deal with on a subtler level. At the next meeting, I was there five minutes early, started on time and closed the meeting five minutes later, apologising to those who had troubled to turn up on time, for their fellow directors' disrespect in thinking they had more valuable things to do. This was a bold strategy to employ when my board was all male, and I was the new kid on the block, but it put a stop to this behaviour immediately. IMy actions were minuted and when we reconvened the whole board were present on time, ready to do their job.

We cannot assume it is only men who may want to sabotage our climb to the top. I am afraid some women are just as culpable, which is a real shame. I believe that as women our power lies in our sense of community and collaboration, which can help build a stronger and better work environment that will, ultimately, be more sustainable. The common perception that female bosses are 'bitches' who don't support you leaves a very bad taste in my mouth.

Choosing to Climb Another Ladder Strategically

Sometimes the choice to change ladders is all about finding a different upward path. Alison, whom I referred to earlier, is one example of how you can get the most from changing career paths in order to step up. She chose to move into a different aspect of the business when she saw a gap she could fill. This move helped her obtain the management role she was being denied because of the company culture. There are many women, and men, who have done the same in the past.

Sasi is a vibrant and talented woman who is now a senior project manager with a large pharmaceutical company. She has been in company management for 19 years. Having started her career as a forensic scientist, she soon realised she wasn't going to get very far in this role.

Sasi left and joined the organisation she still works in. Originally she found herself in a very similar role, but because she took the initiative and trained others as they came in, she ensured she was always up to speed with new systems and anything else important to her role.

As she moved into her supervisory and management roles she found herself working more and more with IT. When the opportunity presented itself, she decided to move into a totally different area, which combined her science skills and IT knowledge. Thus, she moved into project management in the IT area of the business. In this role Sasi's career grew, which would never have happened if she had stayed in her original company.

Sasi and Alison's stories demonstrate that often the best way to advance our careers is to make strategic moves within a company, or move from company to company. Sometimes this will involve stepping sideways onto a new ladder, or even taking a step down on the current or new career ladder in order to reach the highest rung we possibly can in our careers.

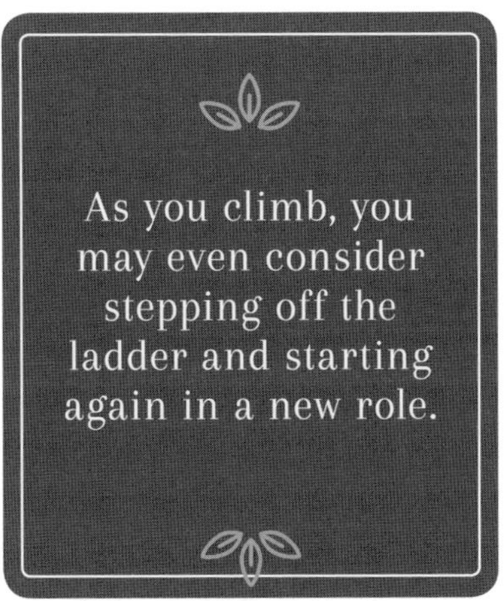
As you climb, you may even consider stepping off the ladder and starting again in a new role.

Susan Colantuono talks about this in her TED X talk entitled *The Career Advice You Probably Didn't Get*. How we contribute to the strategic growth of our business affects our ability to be leaders. The assessment of how we manage our roles has a far greater impact on our future chances of promotion than almost anything else. Generally, men handle this better than women.

You need to look at your career so you understand what needs to be done in order to start climbing the ladder. As you climb, you may even consider stepping off the ladder and starting again in a new role.

Key Strategies to Climb the Ladder

- Using strategies can make a huge contribution if you want to succeed in your career, so you need to be aware of what is happening around you and know how to play company politics.
- Sometimes the best move is to change your role and perhaps your discipline. Having every possible qualification won't necessarily get you there; but applying your skills probably will.
- One of the most important things looked for when considering promoting someone is how they have contributed to the financial and business growth of the organisation.

RUNG 11

Whose Ladder Is It Anyway?

"Passion is what gives us meaning to our lives. It is what allows us to achieve success beyond our wildest imagination. Try to find a career path you have passion for."

—Henry Samueli

Finally, I would like to tell you about how and why I am now standing on my own ladder. At the age of 34 I decided to take a year out from my roles as group human resources manager and executive chairman of the board, to work as national president of Junior Chamber International (JCI) Australia. Doing this meant giving up my six-figure salary and receiving a stipend of about 3,500 Australian dollars to cover travel expenses instead. A lot of travel was involved, so I financed myself. I attended leadership summits at the United Nations in

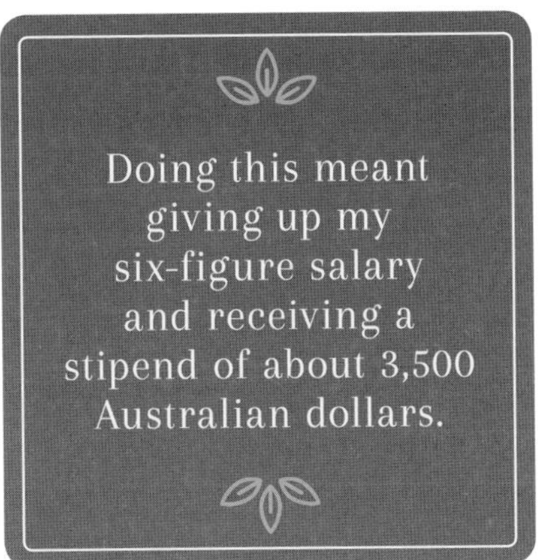
Doing this meant giving up my six-figure salary and receiving a stipend of about 3,500 Australian dollars.

New York, undertook projects in countries such as Bangladesh, and travelled round Australia helping young people in their 20s and 30s to develop their leadership skills and build sustainable communities. It was a wonderful year in which I learned a huge amount and developed my career in a totally different direction.

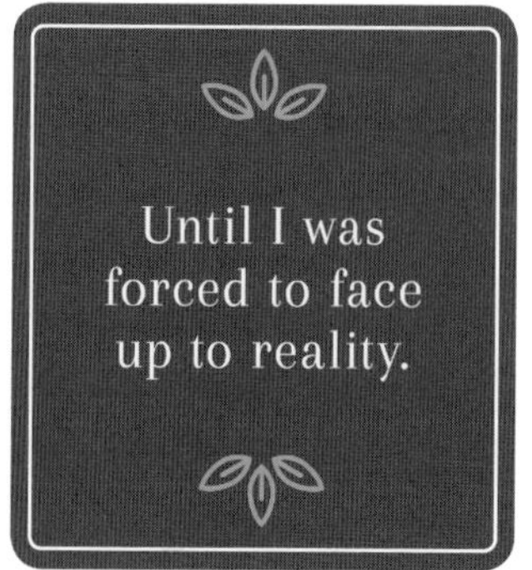
Until I was forced to face up to reality.

My big moment came at the end of the year when it was time to step back into my corporate role. I struggled. Early on in the year I had decided I didn't want to go back to my previous role. It was time to step up into a multinational company role. This was what I had been working towards. I had the Institute of Company Directors Scholarship in my pocket, I still sat on two industry boards and I was a member of the Government Advisory Committee for the state of Victoria. All I had to do was go out and make it happen.

I stalled.

I delayed updating my CV. I had difficulty talking about roles with my connections. I made many excuses, until I was forced to face up to reality – it wasn't my ladder I had been climbing. It just wasn't what I wanted!

I had just spent a year doing something that made me really happy and caused my heart to sing. None of the roles I was looking at filled me with that joy. So I walked away from it all.

I often tell people I hopped on a plane and spent the next 10 years bumming around the world, but this isn't strictly true. I did hop on a plane; I did travel to many places around the world; but I did not bum!

Instead, I set up my own company and found a balance between work and volunteering. As a result I have been lucky enough to live in many different countries, learn about many different cultures and undertake contracts in industries from oil and gas to education.

I have climbed my ladder. I know this because this time it is not just about what I have achieved on paper; this time my heart sings.

I finally realised that I had been climbing everyone else's ladder – my mum's, my dad's and my friends'. I had done what I had been told and actually done it really well. You can do very well following a career others suggest, but to be really happy and successful you also need to have a passion for it.

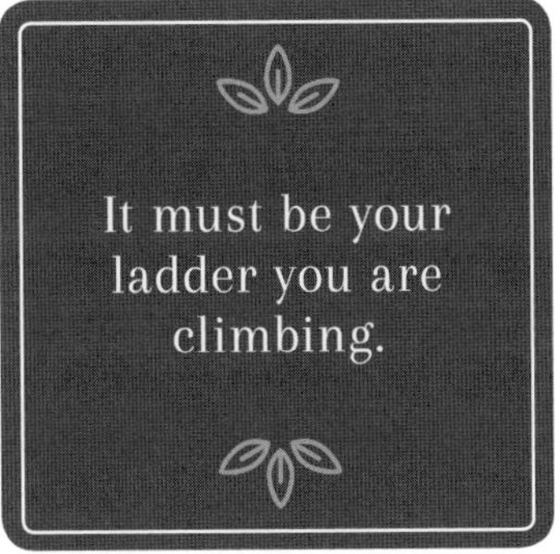
It must be your ladder you are climbing.

Over the past decade I have been lucky enough to work in roles that I am passionate about. The best thing about it is that I want to continue doing so and have stopped looking for ways to move on.

Regardless of your ultimate intention for your career, it must be **your** ladder you are climbing.

Acknowledgements

It seems to me this is often the most difficult part to write for fear of leaving anyone out! I would like to start by thanking the Reverend Heather Widdows, BME. She has been a superstar, with all her help in editing the book. The help was priceless. I am especially thankful that the only big question she had after reading my story was what Tom's reaction was to my mum telling the 'marriage story'. It is easy to see how Tom has grown into the man he is with Heather as one of his guides.

Speaking of the man, I want to thank Tom Widdows, my partner, my rock and my soul mate (although I can see him cringing at those descriptions!). He has been everything you would want in a life partner. Without his support, I may have got to the end eventually, but he made sure I had everything I needed to step up and truly go out, and not only make this book happen but also step out and build my business up to the next level.

To my fellow Empresses (my high level collaboration group – www.empressglobal.com), whilst I cannot name you all, I want to thank some key Empresses for keeping me on track with my book and taking up the challenge: Dr Joanna Martin, Suzanne Dibble, Marianne Page, Heena Thaker, Tressa Henderson, Lynda Holt, Joanna Rawbone, Lucy Whittington and Jennie Lawson. Each of you in your own ways kept me on track, but most of all you believed in me, which helped me stay focused and remember the higher purpose to all this.

To my coach Lynne Elder, you are amazing. Thank you for keeping me on task. I love the way you are able to deal with all the big ideas I have, keep them alive but bring me back to earth in a way that keeps the dream alive. You get me and you help to make it all come together.

To all the amazing women and girls, who helped me draw this book together, some of your stories are mentioned in the pages of this book, others didn't quite make it, but that doesn't mean they were any less valuable. Sometimes it is unfortunate that we have limited space to write things. Thank you to each of you from around the world who took time out to be interviewed by me about your leadership experiences: Alison Reeves, Andrea Mead, Anna Namakula, Annabel Graham, Annik Kindts, Ariana Oluwole, Baya Salmon-Hawk, Carey-Ann Oestreicher, Consuela Dezso, Deanna Radaj, Eva Orban, Janet McConnon, Jemima Vivien, Joie Garrity, Julia Lea, Julia Saurazas, Lalana Zaveri, Lara Khouri, Lejla Softic, Levana, Lisa Lamont, Lisa Rehurek, Margaretha Eriksson, Maria Kathlyn Tan, Nancy Sylvester Ganzekaufer, Nicci Bonfanti, Olwyn Merrit, Patricia Stretton, Sasi Panchal, Selina Boshorin, Shiobhan Costello, Solveig Malik, and Sywlia Korsak.

My best friend Marnie Blakeman, who has supported me all the years we have known each other. You are more a sister to me than a mere friend. I am inspired by you and so fortunate to have you in my life. I still look forward to spending more time in Australia again so we can sit and talk. The fact that you hear me has made all the difference in this book happening, most of all it is the fact that you get me and helped me express myself in those moments I was struggling to make the words come together.

I would like to thank my publisher Gerry Robert, Black Card Books, and the amazing team that worked with me to make this happen. They are impeccable.

I know there are so many others out there that I have not mentioned but you know who you are, and you know that I do thank you from the bottom of my heart (and the soles of my feet). It is a truly motivational feeling knowing there are so many people out there that believe in you.

I want to thank my 'Physics Girls', as you are in my mind. To the amazing girls of Castlemilk High School, who at a time when I was wavering over whether this was the right thing to do, reminded me why it was so important to write this book. To Chloe Elliott, Chloe Greenwood, Jodi Roulston, Pierrette Mayevo, Abbie Campbell and Catherine Lawrence, every time you asked questions in class, came to supported study or just asked if you could sit in my classroom and do some work, you reminded me that it is important to speak up so that the next generation does not have to repeat the same process. I know that each of you is going to fly in your future careers and I am privileged to have been able to be a part of that journey for a short time.

Finally, I want to thank you, my readers. You will take this journey to the next level, and be the ones to make it all happen. Please share your stories with me. I love hearing about the journeys we are all having.

All the best,

The International Stress Management Association[UK]

The International Stress Management Association [ISMAUK] is the lead professional body for workplace and personal Stress Management, well-being and performance.

A registered charity, ISMAUK exists to promote sound knowledge and best practice in stress management, both nationally and internationally.

The work of ISMAUK and its membership includes providing advice to members of the public and employers/organisations.

ISMAUK is the founder of National Stress Awareness Day which takes place on the first Wednesday of November each year.

Website: www.isma.org.uk
Email Address: admin@isma.org.uk
Address: c/o Folds Cottage,
28 Cromford Road, Crich, Derbyshire DE45DJ

Registered Charity Number: 1088103